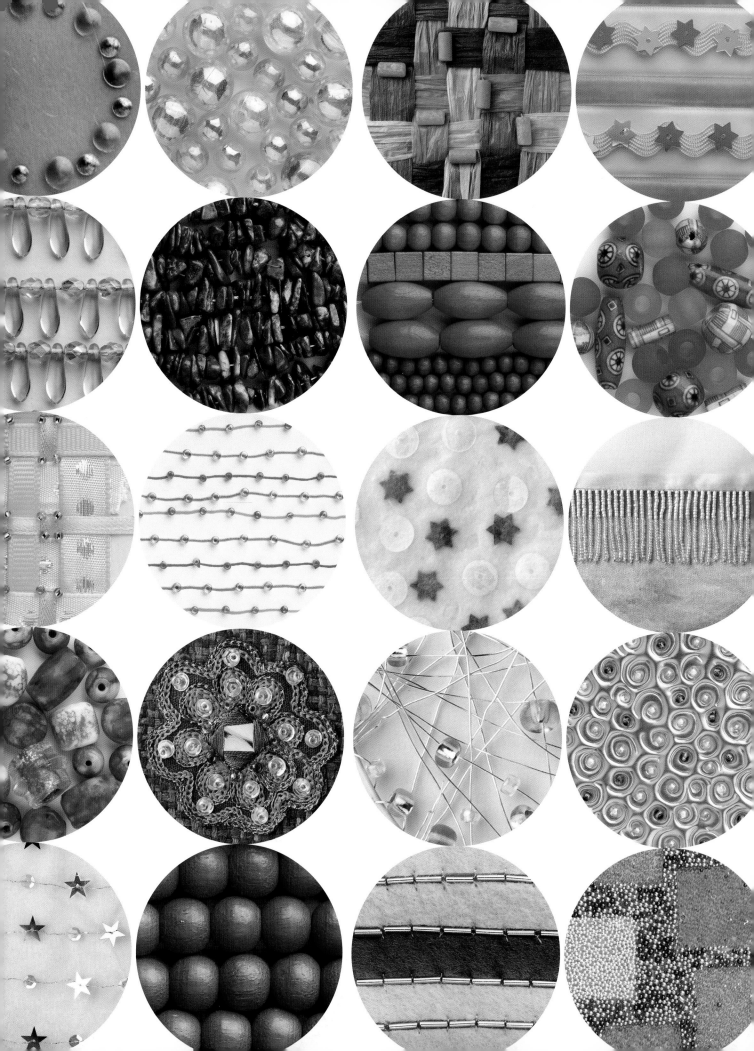

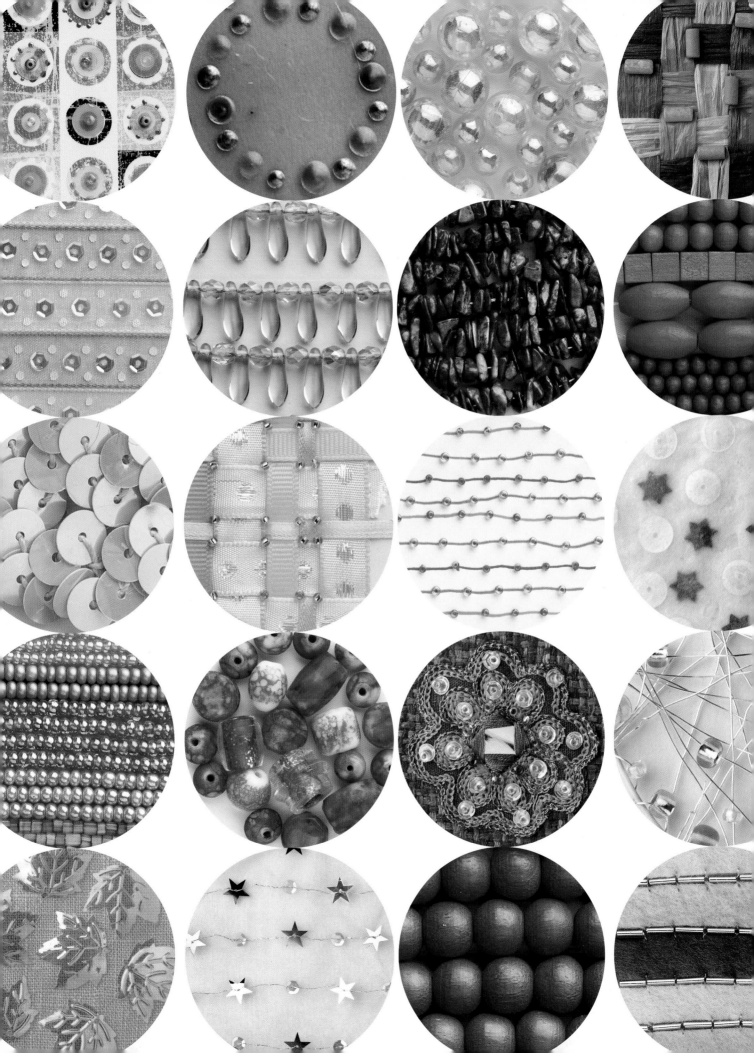

Quick & Clever beading

Dorothy Wood

D&C
David and Charles

A DAVID & CHARLES BOOK
Copyright © David & Charles Limited 2006

David & Charles is an F+W Publications Inc. company
4700 East Galbraith Road
Cincinnati, OH 45236

First published in the UK in 2006

Text and project design copyright © Dorothy Wood 2006

Dorothy Wood has asserted her right to be identified as author of this work
in accordance with the Copyright, Designs and Patents Act, 1988.

A catalogue record for this book is available from the British Library.

ISBN-13: 978-0-7153-2310-6 hardback
ISBN-10: 0-7153-2310-5 hardback

ISBN-13: 978-0-7153-2309-0 paperback
ISBN-10: 0-7153-2309-1 paperback

Printed in China by SNP Leefung
for David & Charles
Brunel House   Newton Abbot   Devon

Executive Editor Cheryl Brown
Editor Jennifer Proverbs
Art Editor Prudence Rogers
Production Controller Ros Napper
Project Editor Lin Clements
Photographer Ginette Chapman

Visit our website at www.davidandcharles.co.uk

David & Charles books are available from all good bookshops; alternatively you can
contact our Orderline on 0870 9908222 or write to us at FREEPOST EX2 110, D&C Direct,
Newton Abbot, TQ12 4ZZ (no stamp required UK only); US customers call 800-289-0963
and Canadian customers call 800-840-5220.

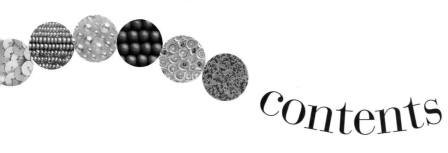

contents

into Aladdin's cave...   14

beads, beads, beads!

Bead shops are a little like Aladdin's Cave – boxes of gorgeous gems seem to cover every surface, almost spilling on to the floor; tempting you with their rich colours and wonderful sparkle.

A good bead shop can be almost intoxicating in its opulence and is certainly one of the most inspiring places to visit. I came upon such a place while on holiday in Paris recently that was a fabulous treasure trove. Inside the décor was rather romantic and old fashioned. Beads of all shapes and sizes were displayed in alcoves, along with ribbons, braids and cords, making me feel like I really was searching through lost treasure. The alcoves were colour co-ordinated to make it as easy as possible to choose a suitable selection of beads. I came away with some beautiful beads, sequins, braids and accessories to add to my collection, and full of inspiration ready to begin this book.

Because beading is often thought of as an enjoyable but time-consuming craft, my aim here was to show quick and clever ways to use the fabulous decorative qualities of beads. This book brings together a diverse range of gorgeous, contemporary projects, which all incorporate beads in some way. Traditional techniques such as bead embroidery and jewellery making are included but the emphasis of each technique is always speed and innovation – plus a dash of style. I've used lush fabrics, gleaming foils and handmade papers in a clever way to create an opulent, encrusted look with just a few beads. Conversely, you will see that ready-made beaded products such as fringing, braids and motifs are easy ways to add lots of lovely beads quickly.

To inspire you to look for imaginative ways to use beads try the chapters focussing on combining craft materials, such as polymer clay and multi-surface paints with beads. This is a book for all bead enthusiasts and crafters alike – to give everyone the opportunity to widen their horizons and to find new and rewarding ways to work with beads.

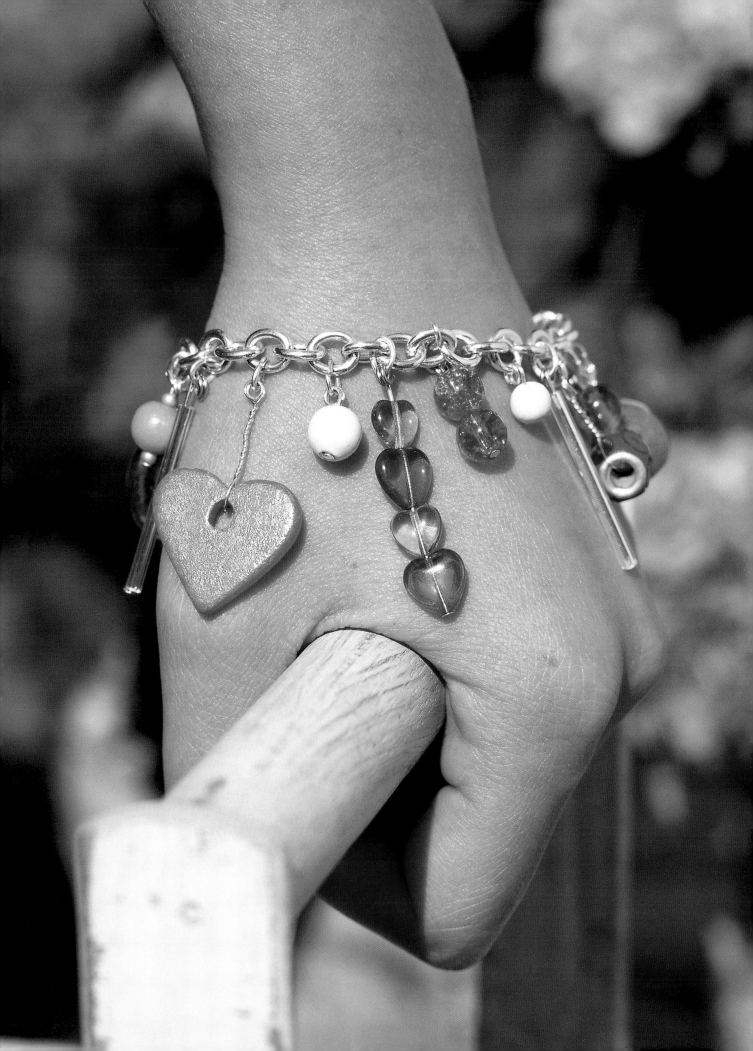

beads & materials

The purpose of this book is to show how easy it is to combine beads with other crafts. The materials described on the following pages are basic items, easily obtained from craft stores and mail-order.

beads

Beads are one of the most attractive embellishments you can buy. They come in all shapes and sizes, from the tiniest seed beads to huge, chunky beads and are readily available from your local beading shop, on-line or by mail order. Larger beads are usually sold singly and smaller beads by weight in a bag or small container. There are all sorts of beads, from cheap and cheerful plastic beads to more expensive semi-precious stones and high quality lamp beads, and so you can always find something to suit the design and your pocket. If you are seeking something a little different look in your local charity shops or car boot sales for old jewellery and other beaded items that can be recycled.

bead shapes and sizes

A quick look in any bead shop will reveal innumerable bead shapes and sizes and it would be an impossible task to list them all here but there are several common shapes and sizes that you can look out for.

Beads can be anything from a flat disc to a perfectly round shape with all sorts of variations in between. Some of the beads have special names – cubes are perfectly square, cone beads have a triangular cross-section and bicone beads look like two pyramids stuck together. Larger beads are measured in millimetres (or fractions of an inch); round beads are measured across the diameter and cylinder beads, which can be round, triangular, oval or square, are measured by length and width. Seed beads or rocailles, which look like tiny donuts, are sold by size, from tiny petite beads (size 15) to larger pebble beads (size 3). Seed beads for general use are usually size 9 or 11. Bugle beads, which are thin glass tubes, are sold by length.

bead holes

All beads, unless they are the tiny, decorative accent beads, have a hole of some sort to feed a thread, wire or cord through. The size of the hole varies and is not always in proportion to the size of the bead. It is a good idea to check the size, especially if you are ordering beads from a catalogue or on-line.

Most bead holes are in the centre but you do get holes off-centre, going through the back like a button, or at one end. Teardrop beads, used to great effect for the candle holder on page 106 are designed to dangle delicately from the narrow end, while shaped beads such as leaves, hearts and stars often have holes going from one end to the other, which makes them ideal for charm bracelets, like the one on page 58.

If your chosen bead has too large a hole try putting a seed bead or other small bead at each end to reduce the size. This holds the bead centrally on the wire or cord.

bead types

Beads are available in a wide range of materials, from plastic and glass to natural materials such as wood, shell, bone and semi-precious stones. The beads you choose will depend on the particular project you want to make and it is not always necessary to buy the most expensive. The beautiful organza and tigertail necklace on page 46 uses affordable plastic beads that are enclosed in a wire-mesh ribbon – glass beads would be too heavy and anything exotic partially hidden. Remember to check if beads are washable if the item is likely to need cleaning at some time. The finish also needs to be durable, especially for bracelets and necklaces that rub on your wrist or neck.

When choosing beads for making a project with polymer clay pick glass beads – plastic beads may melt when the clay is put in the oven to bake.

sequins

Sequins, either round, square or a fancy shape, are cut from shiny plastic or metal foil. They can be flat, cupped to reflect the light or embossed to create a texture. Round or square sequins usually have a hole in the centre and decorative shapes such as leaves or petals have the hole at one end. Larger sequins, known as paillettes, have several holes around the edge. Look out for more unusual sequins sold as a trim. You can easily snip the threads between each sequin and sew or stick them to your project individually.

beaded trims

Beads, like sequins, are not only sold loose but are available ready-made into trimmings, fringing, braids and motifs. It is a more expensive way to buy but the effect is instant and you only buy the beads exactly what you need. The clever use of bead products can be quite effective and with careful design the trimming should become an integral part of the completed project – see the burgundy sequin flower bag on page 64.

ribbons

Ribbons are one of the easiest trimmings to buy, as they are available in such a wide variety of shops. The range of colours and textures is huge – from the sheerest organza to heavyweight twills and velvets and all are suitable for embellishing. Use a pattern or picot edging to dictate where to place the beads or work freely on a plain ribbon. Try using wide ribbons instead of fabric for making small accessories.

fabrics

Beads can be used to embellish all sorts of fabrics. I've used many types of fabric, including silks, felt, velvet, cotton, netting, organza and prints. Choose a weight of fabric to suit the project, using the 'you will need list' in each project as a guide for what to buy. If the fabric you want to use is too lightweight, iron interfacing on the reverse side to add body before sewing on the beads.

papers

There are all sorts of papers that work well with beads. Choose from the wonderful range of handmade papers that tear attractively and add a lovely tactile quality to any design or use a thin card for making gift boxes and cards. You can stick a craft backing paper on to plain card before embellishing with beads (see page 39). Wherever possible I have used standard paper sizes:
A3 – 29.5 x 42cm (11⅝ x 16½in);
A4 – 29.5 x 21cm (11⅝ x 8¼in);
A5 – 21 x 14.8cm (8¼ x 5¾in).

wire

I have used various types of wire in this book because this material works so well with beads. Wire is measured either in mm or by standard wire gauge (swg).

craft wire

The most popular craft wires range from 1mm (19swg) down to 0.375mm (28 swg) and the thinner wires have a larger gauge number. For beading, a good all-round wire to start with is 0.6mm (24swg). Choose from enamelled wire, which has a copper base and is available in a wide range of colours, or silver- and gold-plated wire for a classic finish. Thin wires can be cut with scissors, but wire cutters will needed for thicker wires (see page 11).

memory wire

This is a jewellery wire sold in circles of various diameters for necklaces and bracelets and is called memory wire because it retains its shape. Use a heavyweight wire cutter to cut these hard wires.

tigertail

Tigertail is a tough nylon-covered jewellery wire that is perfect for basic bead stringing and is available as three- or seven-strand types. The core wires range in thickness from 0.12–0.24mm and so there are several thicknesses in each type.

polymer clay

Polymer clay is available in a wide range of colours and there are special finishes such as translucent and glitter. Soft polymer clay is a fairly new product that requires a minimum of kneading before use though it is softer to handle than the traditional classic clay. Press glass or metal beads into the clay before baking or punch tiny holes so that you can string beads over an aperture with fine wire. For using polymer clay, see the Beads & Polymer Clay chapter starting on page 52.

glues and tapes

As the aim of this book is to show quick ways to use beads many of the projects use an adhesive of some sort or another to attach the beads. Beads are three-dimensional, generally without a flat surface, and can be difficult to stick securely. The products listed here are all suitable for a range of surfaces but do look in the 'you will need' lists to see which are suggested for a particular project.

PVA glue

White craft glue is a good basic glue used for several of the projects in the book. Look for PVA glue that has a hi-tack or is labelled strong, and choose one that dries clear. For fine, detailed work decant some glue into a small plastic bottle with a nozzle and attach a metal gutta nib.

superglue

This clear extra-strong glue is ideal for securing single beads or ball ends on to hard surfaces such as wire. The gel version is easier to control: apply a tiny drop to the wire then slide the bead over the glue and leave for a few seconds to dry. If you need a strong glue for larger beads or fitments use an epoxy resin. New versions of this standard workshop glue, which has two components that are mixed together to activate the adhesive, dry much more quickly and some also dry clear.

glue dots

Craft glue dots are ideal for sticking small bead motifs to a smooth surface or for sticking other smooth-surfaced materials like foil. They are available in a range of sizes and different types, such as pop-up glue dots, which raise the motif off the background to give a three-dimensional effect. Mini glue dots are perfect for sticking ribbon.

double-sided adhesive tape

Craft double-sided tape is ideal for sticking paper, card and foil. It can be used to stick accent beads and other tiny beads but the adhesive is not as strong as hi-tack tape and so the beads are likely to rub off in use.

hi-tack tape/film

This extra-strong double-sided tape is available in a range of different widths. It is also sold in sheet form, as hi-tack film, which is ideal for cutting or punching out shapes and covering larger areas. Peel off one layer of backing paper to stick the tape on to the surface and then peel off the top layer to attach the beads. Hi-tack tape is often used for sticking the tiny no-hole beads known as accent beads (see the picture frame on page 74).

dry adhesive tape

Studio Tac is a strong, dry adhesive that is sold on a backing tape. It looks rather like double-sided tape but the adhesive has no carrier and is almost invisible in use once the backing tape is peeled off. Studio Tac is ideal for sticking ribbons, yarn and embellishments on to cards.

multi-surface paints

Although not strictly an adhesive, paints sold in applicator bottles suitable for use on a variety of surfaces as diverse as glass and fabric, are also ideal for sticking beads and sequins. The paint isn't sticky – it simply secures the bead firmly once it has dried. The paints are available in many colours and different finishes such as gloss, metallic, pearl and crystal. Choose a colour to match either the bead or the surface it is being stuck to.

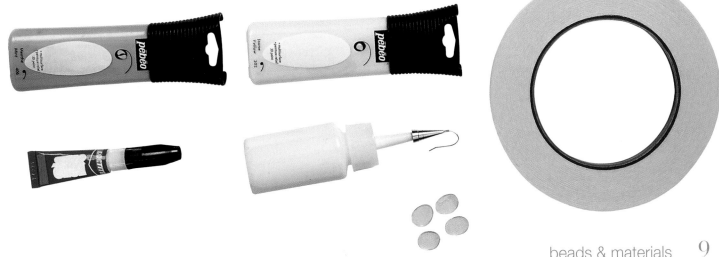

jewellery findings

Findings are the hooks, fastenings and pins that transform beads into jewellery. There are all sorts of styles, from traditional to contemporary, and it is worth searching for unusual fastenings and clasps to match the particular design. Basic findings are silver- or gold-plated but for a special project ask in your local bead shop for sterling silver or even real gold fitments. Look for clasps and fastenings in an appropriate size and shape to make your jewellery look really stunning. Try unusual items too, such as kilt pins (see the card on page 62).

crimp beads and fastenings

Crimp beads are metal tubes or donut shapes that secure threads or beads in a particular position. The crimp is secured by simply squeezing with pliers. Crimp fastenings (calottes) are used to secure and neaten raw ends of cord and thong or even knots at the end of bracelets and necklaces.

earring wires

It is worth paying a little extra for sterling silver earring wires – the designs tend to be more stylish and they are less likely to react with the wearer's skin. There are styles to loop though the ear lobe or screw-on types. Earring wires have a little ring for attaching a head pin or jump ring.

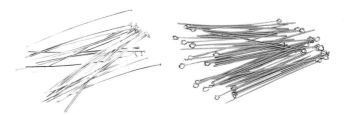

head pins and eye pins

These long lengths of wire look similar but have different uses. A head pin, rather like a long dressmaker's pin is used to make bead charms. You simply add a few beads and make a loop at the top. Eye pins have a loop at the end and are used to make bead links, or the beads can be secured with a crimp bead at the end.

fastenings

Necklace and bracelet fastening come in two parts: spring rings and lobster claws are the basic styles and are available in various sizes, to be used along with a jump ring. Magnetic and cylindrical screw fastenings are ideal for necklaces, whereas more ornate push clasps can be used for bracelets too. Toggle fastenings come in a range of styles and sizes to suit contemporary or traditional jewellery.

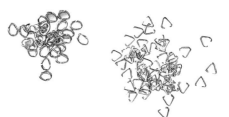

rings and bails

These versatile wire findings have many uses in jewellery making. Rings can be round or oval: soldered rings are more secure for fastenings and jump rings are split so that they can be opened and closed with pliers. Triangular-shaped links are known as bails and are used to hang teardrops and other similar beads.

wire cutters   round-nosed pliers   flat-nosed pliers

jewellery tools

Jewellery and other projects that have wire as a design element will be easier to make with a set of jewellery tools. For ease of use, look for small tools with a spring action.

wire cutters

Many fine wires can be cut to length quite easily with a pair of craft scissors. However, if you are making jewellery or trying to cut wire ends close to a project you will get better results with a pair of wire cutters. Hold the flat edge of the cutters away from the 'tail' of the wire for best results (see below).

round-nosed pliers

The tapered jaws of these pliers are used to make rings of wire. Hold the wire near the top of the jaws to make a small ring and near the base to make a larger ring.

flat-nosed pliers

These are ideal for holding small beads and manipulating wire. Look out for those with a fairly smooth surface on the gripping part of the jaws. If they are too serrated the teeth will damage the wire. Some flat-nosed pliers have a snipe nose for fine work.

Using the right tools can bring a professional finish to your beadwork. Jewellery tools allow you to bend, curl and cut wire more easily.

basic equipment

Each project in the book has a list of the equipment you will need. If you are a keen crafter it is likely that you will have most things in your toolbox already as nothing is particularly specialized. People new to crafting and beadwork can assemble a basic kit (see below) and then, at a later date, acquire tools and equipment that you will need only occasionally.

basic kit

cutting mat (1), craft knife (2) and metal-edged ruler (3)

These three items are essential if you are a keen crafter. A self-seal cutting mat protects your work surface and a metal-edged ruler is safer to use with craft knives. Change your knife blade often, as a sharp blade is safer than a blunt one and produces a better result. Use pointed blades for fine or curved work and a flat blade for straight cutting on card.

scissors (4)

Keep separate scissors for craft and fabric work. Paper blunts scissors very quickly and you will find they no longer cut fabric cleanly. Use a small pair of embroidery scissors for close work and a larger pair for cutting fabric. Inexpensive multi-packs of scissors are ideal for craftwork and allow you to use the correct size for the task in hand.

pens, pencils and markers (5)

Choose your method of marking depending on the material you are using and whether the mark will be visible once the project is finished. A vanishing embroidery marker is ideal for fabric, while a pencil can be erased from paper and card.

bone folder (6) and embossing tools (7)

If you are going to fold card frequently a bone folder or embossing tool is essential for a professional finish.

needles and threads (8)

When sewing, choose a needle that matches the thickness of the thread you are using. When attaching beads, check that the beads will pass over the eye of the needle – you may need to use a thinner beading needle. Use matching sewing thread for basic sewing.

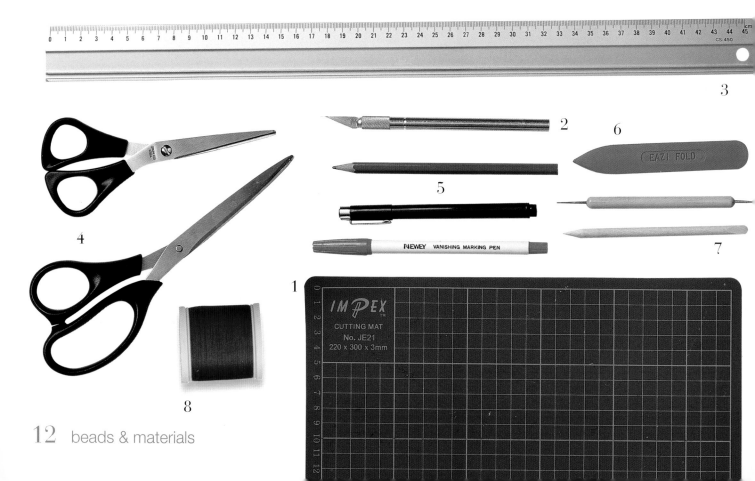

basic techniques

As the name of the book suggests, I have avoided lengthy and complicated techniques. The project instructions contain all you need to know, but for those new to beadwork this page shows how to attach beads by sewing. This can be done in various ways but for this book you only need to know how to attach a single bead and how to sew beads on in lines or patterns.

sewing beads on individually

When sewing beads individually it is essential to secure the thread carefully on the reverse side when beginning and finishing off. Use a strong thread such as quilting thread, or a double thickness of sewing cotton.

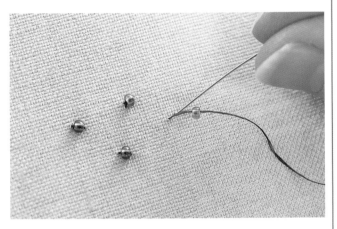

one It is advisable to go through each bead twice to secure it. This makes it less likely the bead will fall off and also prevents the thread pulling through if the beads are spaced out.

two When stitching larger beads, space the two threads out in the hole so that the bead is held firmly in position. For extra security, take a tiny backstitch on the reverse side before sewing on the next bead.

sewing beads with backstitch

Backstitch can be used to add individual beads or several at a time. Only pick up one or two beads to follow a curved line but pick up more the straighter the line, taking the needle back through the last bead each time.

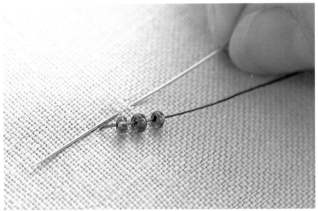

one Pick up three beads and let them drop down to where the thread emerges. Put the needle back through the fabric at the end of the three beads. Take a small backstitch and bring the needle out between the last two beads.

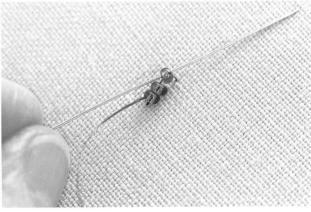

two Put the needle back through the last bead and then pick up another three beads ready to begin again. When a line of beads is complete, secure on the back of the work with a few tiny backstitches.

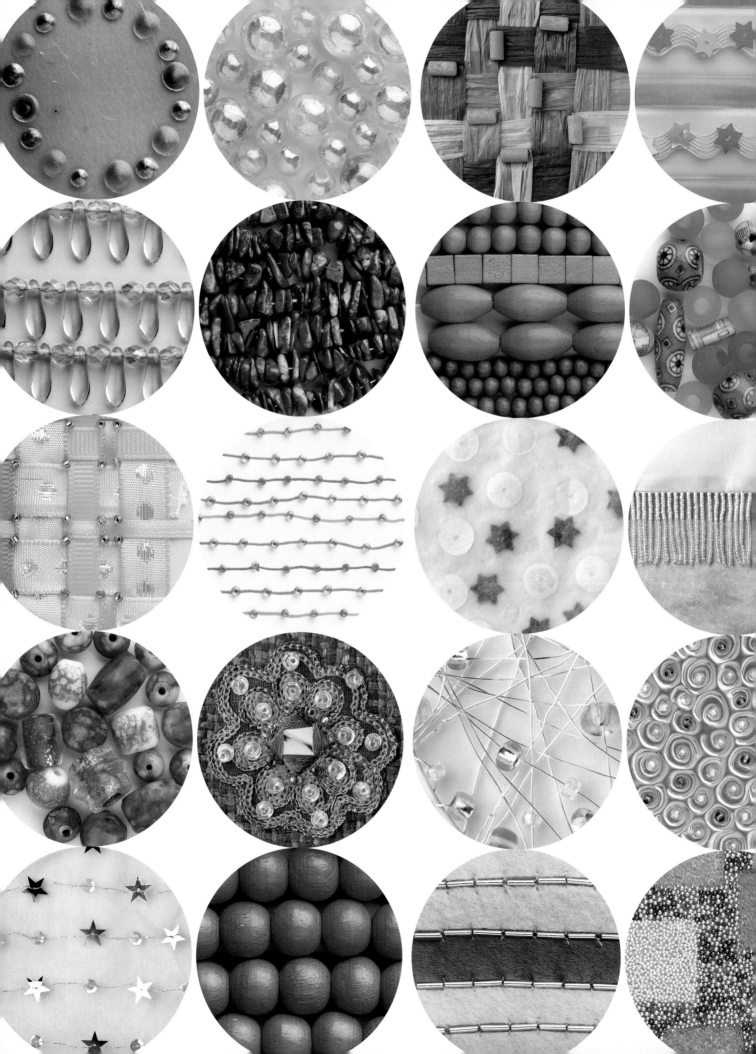

into Aladdin's cave...

This book brings together a diverse collection of attractive and easy to make projects that incorporate beads in a variety of ways. Traditional techniques such as jewellery making and bead embroidery are included, as well as ways to use beads with interesting materials like polymer clay, metal foil and glass. The clear instructions for each project are easy to follow whether you are a novice or an experienced crafter and any templates that you need are reproduced full size on pages 112–115.

The projects are grouped together according to the materials used: the main projects are illustrated with step-by-step photographs, and the two variation ideas that follow have clear stepped instructions. Most of the techniques you will need are quick and simple ones and are described within the projects. There is also a colourful side panel, which provides additional inspiration for the particular craft material or type of bead that is the chapter focus. This panel will inspire you by giving some idea of what is available – perhaps a range of colours, different shapes and sizes of beads or alternative ways to use beads.

The projects are many and varied: there are ideas for the home, such as a bead-fringed cushion, a pretty lampshade and a stylish photo frame. There are also delightful ideas to give as gifts, like a pot-pourri sachet and a felt journal, as well as lots of jewellery and accessories you just won't want to give away. There are 55 different projects to choose from – a cornucopia of delights for the bead enthusiast and keen crafter alike.

bead strings

Bead strings are a great way to add a lot of beads to a design quickly, as the beads come ready threaded on a strong string.

beaded fruit

Pincraft – where beads are attached to polystyrene shapes with pins – is an attractive way to make a decorative ornament although it can be rather time consuming as you have to add the beads and sequins individually. These stunning beaded fruits have a similar effect but are made much more quickly using beads pre-strung on thread: you simply wrap the bead strings around the artificial fruit (which has been covered in a tacky tape) until it is covered. Pears are an easy shape to start with but you could make a whole bowl of different fruits such as apples, bananas and oranges.

right When beading fruit, choose strings of pearls in silver, grey and white for a special occasion or small beads in bright realistic colours for a fun display.

you will need... (for three pears)

- ✓ Three artificial pears
- ✓ 6mm (¼in) wide high-tack double-sided tape

- ✓ 2,000 silver pearls on strings
- ✓ 2,000 grey pearls on strings
- ✓ 2,000 white pearls on strings

quick & clever Ask in your local bead store for beads available on strings – the beads often arrive from wholesalers on strings and there may be some in the store room.

one Using narrow high-tack double-sided tape, stick a strip of tape from the top of the fruit down to the bottom. Stick three more strips evenly spaced so that the pear is marked in quarters.

two Stick further strips halfway between each of the previous strips. Continue working around the pear, sticking strips in the gaps until the fruit is completely covered in tape. Occasional small gaps will not be a problem.

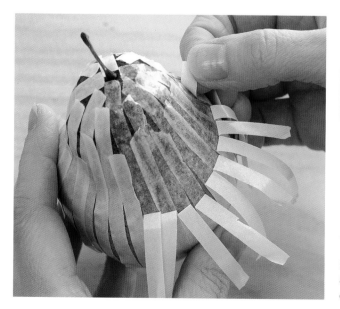

three Peel the backing paper from the tape so it comes about halfway down and crease each end to keep it out of the way.

four Untie the silver pearl strings and separate each of the strands. Beginning at the top of the pear stick the thread to the tape and coil the first few pearls around the stalk. Continue wrapping the bead string around the fruit so there are no gaps between the rows.

quick & clever Don't touch the exposed double-sided tape with your fingers or lay it down on a fabric surface as it will lose some of its tackiness and not give such good results.

five At the end of the bead string, stick the thread end down from the last bead and then join on another string by feeding the new thread behind the last four pearls. Make sure the pearl strings butt together and then trim the thread ends. Continue adding beads down to the halfway mark.

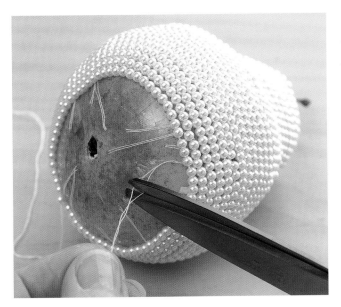

six Peel off the remaining backing paper from the tape. Turn the pear upside down and continue adding bead strings. As you get further down, you may need to add a second layer of double-sided tape to cover some of the thread ends so that the beads will stick. Continue adding bead strings until the pear is completely covered.

Make two more pears in the same way using the grey and white pearls.

quick & clever If the pears are going to rest on their sides when on display, stick a larger brown bead at the round end to make the pear look more realistic.

There is a wide selection of beads available on strings – the examples shown left are just a few of the luscious beads sold this way, including seed beads, pearls, wood beads and semi-precious stones. Wood beads are inexpensive and available in attractive shapes, while pearls are often dipped and coloured to order. The many gorgeous shades are sure to inspire you to create fabulous projects of your own.

round 'n' round

Bead strings are perfect for decorating stationery, from little notepads to large photo albums. This book has a spiral theme using glass seed beads, but you could make a wedding album look special with some romantic pearl strings.

you will need...

✓ Notebook – this one is 10 x 10cm (4 x 4in)

✓ Strings of glass seed beads in pink, lilac and rainbow

✓ Strong PVA glue with fine nozzle

✓ Tacky tape sheet

one Apply a line of rainbow beads to the cover near the spine by cutting the bead string to length, leaving about 1cm (⅜in) of thread at each end. Stick the thread ends on the reverse side of the cover. Repeat with lilac beads.

two To make the loops, draw the pattern with a thin line of PVA glue. Lay the pink bead string on top, letting the beads separate slightly where they overlap and tucking the exposed string between the beads using a pin.

three To make the spiral bead pattern, stick a 4cm (1½in) diameter circle of tacky tape on the cover. Beginning in the middle with pink beads, stick about 1cm (⅜in) of thread on the tape and coil. To change colour, feed the thread end of the next string behind a few beads, and continue.

four Cut the last bead string leaving at least 1cm (⅜in) of thread to tuck under the last few beads so that it is stuck securely in place.

wave hello!

This speedy design uses waves of bead strings to make a card for any occasion. Use beads of similar size in toning colours.

quick & clever Choose paper that tones with the beads. Pads of co-ordinating plain, patterned and vellum papers make this simple.

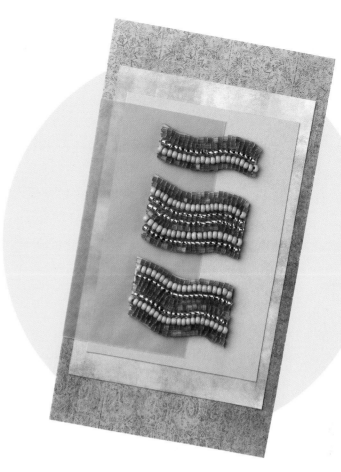

you will need...

✓ Backing papers
✓ Card stock, A4 (US letter) size
✓ Small quantities of lilac glass seed beads: silver-lined, hex, opaque and transparent
✓ Double-sided adhesive tape
✓ Beading needle and strong thread

try this ....
Make a matching tag in a similar way to the card, using just one bead panel.

one Thread the needle and fold a bit of tape over the end to prevent beads escaping. Thread the beads a few at a time until you have about 5cm (2in) of beads. Repeat with the other co-ordinating beads.

two Cut a 4cm (1½in) wide strip of card. Cover one side with double-sided tape. Stick a narrower strip down the edges of the reverse.

three Stick the thread end to the taped edges. Let the bead string fall to the right side in a wavy line. Take any excess beads to the reverse side. Stick the thread on to the tape and trim any excess.

four Stick on further bead strings to make a wavy panel 2–4cm (¾–1½in) wide. Carefully cut the card above and below the beads. Make two more panels on the same strip and cut out.

five Make a single-fold card from card stock; stick rectangles of co-ordinating backing papers on to the front. Attach the bead panels with double-sided tape.

quick & clever There are many products ideal for sticking beads. Tacky tape is a very strong double-sided tape, and tacky tape foil is a sheet version that can be punched or cut into shapes.

bead fringing

Choose from a huge range of beautiful bead fringing to add instant elegance to cushions, lampshades and other household items.

scatter cushion

This cushion has been made from scratch with fabric but it is quite possible to add bead fringing to a ready-made cushion to create an almost instant luxurious finishing touch. Whether adding bead fringing to a ready-made item or making it, try out different bead fringings on the actual fabric to see what looks best. As beads are often translucent, they will take on the colour of the background fabric and can get lost on the wrong colour. As sewing machines will not stitch over beads, unravel some strands inside the seam allowance and sew in the thread end or glue securely to prevent beads falling off.

The cushion shown is 30cm (12in) square.

right Choose interesting fabrics, such as richly printed silk for the flap to co-ordinate with the colour and style of the bead fringing and contrast attractively with the main fabric.

you will need...

- ✓ Bead fringing 32cm (12½in)
- ✓ Silk 20 x 32cm (7¾ x 12½in)
- ✓ Main fabric 32 x 64cm (12½ x 25in)
- ✓ Lining fabric 45 x 32cm (18 x 12½in)
- ✓ Cushion pad 30cm (12in) square
- ✓ Sewing and tacking (basting) thread
- ✓ Dressmaker's pins

one Cut two pieces of main fabric, 32 x 32cm (12½ x 12½in). Cut one piece of silk, 8 x 32cm (3¼ x 12½in) and another, 11 x 32cm (4½ x 12½in). Pin the two pieces of silk right sides together and machine stitch down one long side. Allow 1.5cm (⅝in) for seam allowances. Pin one of the main fabric panels to the deeper silk panel and machine stitch the seam. Press the seams open.

quick & clever Look in your local home-style store for interesting tablemats or napkins made in unusual fabrics that could be used for this cushion.

two Cut a 32cm (12½in) length of bead fringing that has the same bead at each end. Carefully remove any beads inside the seam allowance at both ends and pin the fringe along the edge of the narrow silk panel so that the ribbon/tape is next to the cut edge. Tack (baste) along the edge of the fringing to secure it.

quick & clever If the bead fringing is on an attractive tape or braid you can simply make the cushion and attach the bead fringing to the flap.

three
Cut a 45 x 32cm (18 x 12½in) piece of lining fabric. Lay this on top of the prepared panel with right sides together and pin in position. The silk panel will become the flap of the cushion so tack (baste) the top of the cushion panel from the bottom seam of the silk panel around to the bottom seam on the other side. Fit a zipper foot on the sewing machine and stitch the side seams as tacked and across the top as close as possible to the edge of the fringing.

four
Snip into the seam allowance at the bottom of the machine stitching at both sides. Trim the flap seams and across the corners. Turn the flap through, ease out the corners and press.

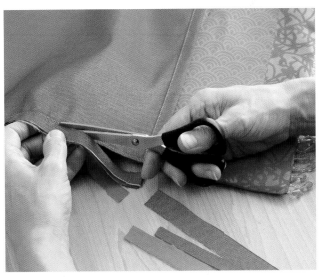

five
Turn under 6mm (¼in) and then 1.25cm (½in) along one edge of the remaining main fabric panel and machine stitch. Pin with right sides together so that the hemmed edge is level with the bottom edge of the flap.

six
Machine stitch around the side and bottom seams. Zigzag the seam and trim close to the stitching. Turn the cushion cover through, ease out the corners and press. Insert a cushion pad to finish.

Bead fringing has long been available for soft furnishing but lighter weight versions are now on sale in dress fabric departments and shops selling ribbons. Remember to ask if there are any catalogues – you will be amazed at the variety of styles available in a wide range of different beads. Some are expensive, but you may be inspired to create fringing of your own, especially if you only need a short length.

sweet heart

Narrow fringing is ideal for decorating the edge of a small cushion or sachet. It is usually easier to buy the fringing first and then select matching fabric and embellishments, such as these gorgeous heart buttons.

quick & clever Instead of putting pot-pourri inside the cushion, add a few drops of fragrance oil on the back to keep it smelling sweet.

you will need...

✓ Pink silk, two squares 15cm (6in)

✓ Pale pink silk offcut

✓ Pink netting 15cm (6in) square

✓ Fusible bonding web

✓ Bead fringing 60cm (24in)

✓ Three heart buttons

✓ Polyester stuffing

✓ Pot-pourri sachet

quick & clever Rather than searching for similar beads, unravel a short length of bead fringe and use the loose beads.

one Iron a 7cm (2¾in) square of pale pink silk on to fusible bonding web. Draw a 5cm (2in) square on the backing paper and cut out the shape. Peel off the backing paper, place in the centre of a large pink square and fuse the layers together with a warm iron.

two Lay the 15cm (6in) square of pink net on top of the bonded silk squares and tack (baste) around the edge. Sew seed beads every 3–4mm (⅛in) around the edge of the small square. Sew three translucent heart buttons in the centre of the small square.

three Remove about 1.25cm (½in) of fringing from the end of the tape. Pin the fringing around the edge of the embellished square, snipping into the tape at each corner. Tack the tape in place and then lay the second 15cm (6in) silk square on the right side. With matching sewing thread, stitch around the edge using a zipper foot to stitch close to the beads, leaving a gap on one side. Trim across the corners and turn through. Ease out the corners, press and stuff with polyester stuffing and pot-pourri. Slipstitch the gap to finish.

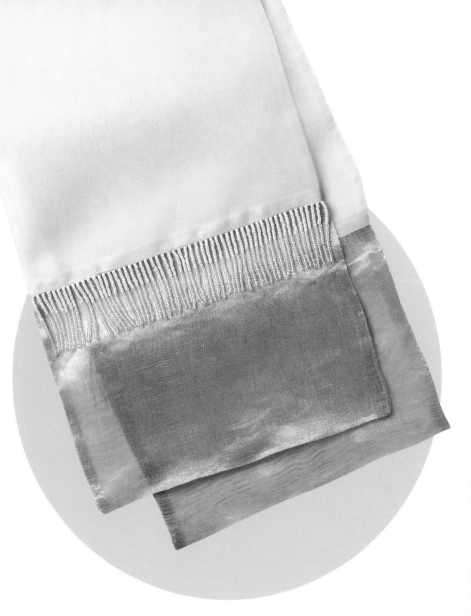

sheer 'n' swinging

Make a gorgeous scarf in sheer silk organza to match your favourite evening outfit and add a touch of luxury with some subtly shaded bead fringing.

quick & clever Bead fringing that has an attractive braid or tape can be attached quite easily to a ready-made scarf. Simply fold under the ends and stitch by hand or machine.

you will need...

- ✓ Cream organza 46 x 112cm (18 x 44in)
- ✓ Metallic cream organza 46 x 30cm (18 x 12in)
- ✓ Bead fringing 46cm (18in)

one Cut two pieces of cream organza 23 x 112cm (9 x 44in) and two pieces of metallic organza 23 x 30cm (9 x 12in). Cut two 23cm (9in) lengths of bead fringing. Carefully remove two or three strands from each end to leave 20cm (8in) of fringing in the middle. Make sure the remaining fringing is quite secure.

two Pin a length of bead fringing along both short ends of one piece of cream organza so that the tape is near the raw edge. Using a zipper foot on your sewing machine and matching sewing thread, stitch as close as possible to the beads. Pin a piece of metallic organza over the bead fringe and machine stitch the seam again.

three Pin the second piece of cream organza to the free end of the two pieces of metallic organza (so it makes a tube), making sure all seams are on the outside, and machine stitch. Trim all seams to 6mm (¼in) and press towards the metallic organza.

four Fold the scarf so that the seams match and pin the side seams. Machine stitch the side seams leaving a gap on one side for turning through. Trim the seams to 6mm (¼in) and turn through. Ease out the corners, press the edges and slipstitch the gap.

beads & sequins

Mix and match different bead and sequin trimmings to add instant glamour to fabric, using several rows together to create a strong impact.

dolly bag

The dolly or Dorothy bag is a classic shape that can be brought bang up to date by making it in a rich coloured silk embellished with a funky sequin trim. The sequin embellishment makes more impact as a wider band created from three rows of sequin trim linked together with a luxury sheer ribbon in a toning colour. If you made the bag in pale cream, ivory or pastel shades, it would be ideal for a bride or a bridesmaid. This dolly bag is approximately 16cm (6½in) tall, excluding ribbon handle.

right Choose plain and fancy sequin trims to embellish a simple dolly bag. This classic design is the ideal size for evening occasion or a special event.

you will need...

- ✓ Turquoise silk dupion 32 x 36cm (12½ x 14½in)
- ✓ Medium weight iron-on interfacing 32 x 36cm (12½ x 14½in)
- ✓ Lining fabric 32 x 29cm (12½ x 11½in)
- ✓ Decorative sequin trim 64cm (25in)
- ✓ Plain sequin trim 32cm (12½in)
- ✓ Sheer ribbon 64cm (25in) of 1.5cm (⅝in)
- ✓ Turquoise satin ribbon 112cm (44in) of 7mm (¼in) wide

one Cut a piece of silk dupion 25 x 32cm (10 x 12½in). Cut one piece of interfacing 15 x 32cm (6 x 12½in) and another 9 x 32cm (3½ x 12½in). Iron the two pieces of interfacing, one on top of the other, along the longest edge of the silk dupion.

two Cut the sheer ribbon in half and pin one piece 5cm (2in) from the bottom edge of the bag panel, as shown. Leave a 1.25cm (½in) gap and pin the second piece in place. Catch down the ribbon with tiny stitches along both edges.

three Lay the plain sequin trim between the ribbons and attach it by sewing invisibly through the sequins. Cut the decorative sequin trim in half and sew one piece to each outside edge of the ribbons.

four Measure 9.5cm (3¾in) from the top edge in the centre of the bag panel and mark the position with a pin. Iron a 5cm (2in) square of interfacing on the reverse side with the pin mark in the centre. Tack (baste) the position of two horizontal 1.25cm (½in) buttonholes on the right side either side of the pin. Set the machine to the buttonhole setting and make two buttonholes. Snip along the slit to open the buttonholes.

quick & clever If your sewing machine doesn't make buttonholes, just feed the ribbon tie through the fabric between the casing lines using a large needle.

five Fold the bag panel with right sides together and stitch the back seam to create a tube. Cut an 11cm (4¼in) circle from silk dupion and two circles the same size from interfacing. Iron the interfacing to the reverse side of the silk. Mark the bottom of the bag tube and the circle in quarters with notches. Pin the circle into the bottom of the bag, matching the notches. Tack and then machine stitch together.

quick & clever To reduce bulk on the back seam of the bag, cut away the sequins from the trim inside the seam allowance.

six Turn down the top edge of the bag by 5cm (2in) and press. Machine stitch a 1cm (⅜in) casing 3cm (1¼in) from the top edge. Make a lining in the same way as the bag, from an 18 x 32cm (7 x 12½in) piece of lining and 11cm (4⁵⁄₁₆in) circle. Turn down the top edge and press.

seven For the bag handle, cut a 35cm (14in) length of satin ribbon and sew the ends securely on the inside of the bag, level with the lower casing line. Turn the bag outside in and pull on the lining. Pin along the lower edge of the casing and slipstitch in place. Thread a 76cm (30in) length of satin ribbon through one buttonhole on the casing line and back out the other. Trim the ribbon ends at an angle, then pull up and tie in a bow.

There are all sorts of bead and sequin trims available from dress and soft furnishing stores, so only a few samples can be shown here. Sequin trimmings are versatile; they can be used singly or with several toning or matching bands together to create a wider border. Bead trimming is usually created on a ribbon base, either sheer or plain, in a range of widths.

funky frame

This little frame looks like it has taken hours to make – the secret is to use a heavy bead trim and then fill in the background with spare seed beads from the trim for a co-ordinated look.

quick & clever Buy a ready-made fabric-covered frame then add a bead trim and a few spare beads to embellish it.

you will need...

- ✓ A4 (US letter) sheet of stiff card
- ✓ Closely woven fabric 16cm (6½in) square
- ✓ Thin wadding (batting) 13cm (5in) square
- ✓ Craft knife and ruler
- ✓ Double-sided tape
- ✓ Bead trim 0.5m (½yd)
- ✓ Assorted seed beads

one Cut a 13cm (5in) square of stiff card and mark a 3cm (1¼in) border all round. Cut out the centre aperture with a craft knife. Cover the card frame with thin wadding (batting) and cut out the aperture.

two Position the card frame face down in the centre of a 16cm (6½in) piece of fabric. Stick double-sided tape around the inner and outer edges of the card frame and stretch the outside fabric over the edges, mitring the corners neatly. Cut into each corner of the aperture and stretch the flaps on to the tape.

three Cut the bead trim to fit down the centre of each side of the frame. Turn under raw edges and attach with double-sided tape. Sew in place with tiny stitches and fill in the corners with large beads. Sew single seed beads randomly over the front of the frame.

four Cut a 12.5cm (5in) square of card for the back of the frame. Stick a photo behind the aperture and then stick the backing in place. Attach a hanger or cut a 4 x 12cm (1½ x 4¾in) strip of card, score 4cm (1½in) from the top, fold slightly and then stick on the back of the frame for a stand.

shades of apricot

Give a small lampshade a new lease of life with a fresh cover and an unusual bead trim. This little lamp has been re-covered with sinamay, a mesh-like hat-making material, and then decorated with two toning sequin trims. Look for something special – you won't need much to go around a small shade. This shade is about 14cm (5½in) across its widest part.

quick & clever If the shade doesn't need re-covering, you can create a really quick new look by just sticking on a matching bead trim and a few random sequins or beads.

you will need...

✓ Natural sinamay 0.3m (⅓yd)
✓ Apricot rose-shaped sequin trim 0.5m (½yd)
✓ Apricot elasticated sequin trim 0.5m (½yd)
✓ 6mm (¼in) wide hi-tack tape
✓ Clear fabric glue

one Remove the old cover from the lampshade. Lay the lampshade on a sheet of paper and wrap around. Crease along the top and bottom edges to mark the shape. Mark the back seam and then cut out to create a pattern. Cutting 2.5cm (1in) outside the paper pattern, cut two pieces of sinamay so that the straight grain is down one of the straight edges of the pattern each time.

two Stick tacky tape down one of the spars of the shade and around the inside of the frame at the top and bottom edges. Peel off the backing paper from the spar tape and stick a piece of sinamay to it. Apply a second length of tape down the edge of the sinamay and then wrap the fabric round the shade. Trim the excess around the top and bottom edges.

three Stick the second layer of sinamay over the top in the same way. This time trim it to 1.25cm (½in) above and below the frame. Peel off the backing tape and ease the sinamay on to the tape on the inside. Stick two or three lengths of tacky tape around the bottom of the shade (the width will depend on your trim).

four Stick the rose trim around the bottom edge and cut to length. Stretch the elasticated trim on to the tape so that it makes a gentle wavy line. Cut separate rose motifs from the trim and stick randomly over the shade with fabric glue. Stick a few apricot sequins in between to finish.

beads & paints

Multi-Surface paints not only embellish surfaces and form designs but also are an ideal medium for sticking beads on to a range of materials.

cocktail fizz

At one time glass paints would have been the only suitable product for creating the bright, jazzy design on these cocktail glasses but new paints have been developed that can be used on a variety of different surfaces. Because of its good adhesive quality, the paint is ideal not only for creating the design but also to stick the beads. The paints (see page 9) are designed to create a three-dimensional effect with a slightly raised surface and come in a container with a medium nozzle. For greater control when making finer lines, you could attach a metal nozzle like the ones used for silk painting.

right For a summer party paint the cocktail glasses bright gloss colours or try pastel pearl paint for a wedding or subtle metallic colours for a Christmas design.

you will need...

- ✓ Two cocktail glasses
- ✓ Multi-surface gloss paints in bright yellow, bright red, cinnamon and pink
- ✓ Tracing paper and pencil

- ✓ Fine black pen
- ✓ 0.5mm (size 5) gutta nib
- ✓ Size 9 seed beads in red, pink, orange and yellow
- ✓ Masking tape

one Trace the outline of the large template on page 114 on to tracing paper and cut out as a circle. Check that the shape fits inside your particular glass and adjust if required. Go over the outline with a fine black pen. Tape the template into a cone shape and secure inside the glass with masking tape.

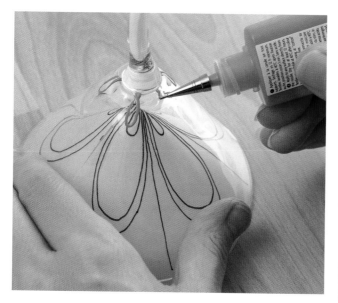

two Fit the gutta nib on to the tip of the orange gloss paint. Turn the glass upside down on a flat surface and draw the small loops out from the top of the stem. Turn the glass round to face you each time you draw a loop as the thickness of the stem distorts the pattern slightly.

three Fit a nib on the yellow and pink gloss paints and draw the larger loops. Finally, draw fine straight lines in red between the petals and add a dot of red paint at the end of each line.

quick & clever The drying time of multi-surface paint depends on the room temperature and the thickness of the line; you need to add the beads before it begins to dry.

✓ Dressmaker's pin

✓ Paintbrush

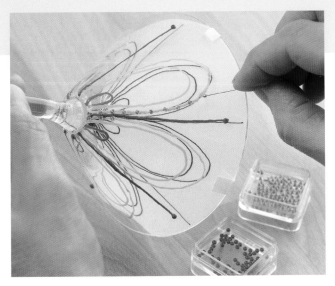

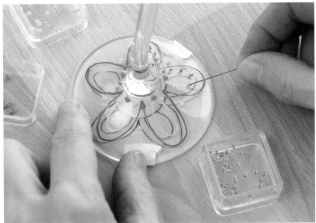

four Choose a selection of seed beads to match or tone with the colours of the multi-surface paints. Use a dressmaker's pin to lift the seed beads on to the paint. Space the beads along the length of each petal and put one at the end of each line. Add a few dots of orange paint and some orange beads to complete the design.

quick & clever Try to keep the dressmaker's pin clean, so that the bead just drops off the end on to the paint line.

five Trace the base template on page 114 on to a piece of tracing paper and cut out to the size of your glass. Stick in place under the base. Stand the glass on the work surface and draw in the paint lines as before then decorate with seed beads.

six Leave the glass overnight to dry. To finish the design, squeeze a small quantity of pink gloss paint into a container, add a little red to darken and then paint the stem with a thin even coat. Leave overnight to dry again.

Multi-surface paints are a versatile product designed to stick to surfaces as diverse as wood, fabric, metal and glass. They are available in different finishes such as gloss, metallic, pearl and crystal, each with a distinctive colour range. The paint has good adhesive qualities and is ideal for attaching beads, sequins and other embellishments.

sparkly bauble

Transform glass baubles with a star motif and embellish with tiny beads and sequins to create a unique decoration. Choose a paint type and colour to match the bauble for a subtle effect or contrasting colours for a bolder look.

quick & clever It's quicker to make several baubles at once – have a few egg cups handy to leave them to dry between stages.

you will need...

- ✓ Metallic multi-surface paints in pink and lilac
- ✓ Purple glass bauble
- ✓ Two 0.5mm (size 5) gutta nozzles
- ✓ Size 9 seed beads in rainbow and lilac
- ✓ Translucent sequins 8mm (⁵/₁₆in)
- ✓ Dressmaker's pin or fine tweezers
- ✓ Lilac organza ribbon 9mm (³/₈in) wide for a hanger
- ✓ Egg cup

one Balance the bauble on an egg cup so the hanging fitment is upwards. Fit a fine nozzle on to the paint applicator and draw a star shape on the bauble near to the hanging fitment. Make some of the 'legs' of the star a little shorter than others.

two Using a pin or fine tweezers, drop a translucent sequin on the end of the shorter 'legs'. Apply a small drop of paint in the centre of each sequin and then drop a rainbow seed bead in the middle using a pin or tweezers.

three Stick lilac beads on the end of the longer 'legs' and a rainbow bead in the centre. Make one or two other stars on the bauble where you can reach and then leave to dry. Balance the bauble on the egg cup upside down and complete the design. Once dry tie on an organza ribbon.

quick & clever It can be tricky working on a round surface so try out the design on scrap paper or acetate before you begin.

dotty greetings

Use the bold pattern of a decorative backing paper to inspire the design for an unusual greetings card suitable for any occasion. If you can't find paper with a circle motif, cut circles or rings from matching plain paper and stick on the card or tag, ready to decorate.

quick
&
clever
You could write a greeting, such as 'with love' or 'happy birthday' in a plain area of the card using the multi-surface paints.

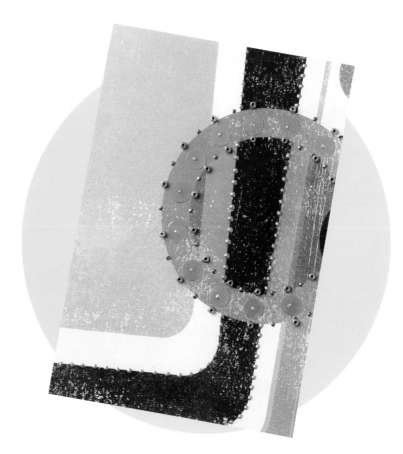

you will need...

✓ Sheet of lilac card

✓ Sheet of decorative backing paper

✓ Metallic multi-surface paint in pale gold and pink-gold

✓ Two 0.5mm (size 5) metal nozzles

✓ Peach sequins 8mm (⁵⁄₁₆in)

✓ Size 9 pinky-lilac seed beads

✓ Dressmaker's pin or tweezers

✓ Double-sided tape

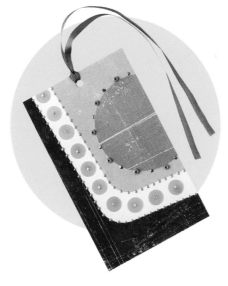

one Cut a 20 x 14.5cm (8 x 5¾in) piece of lilac card. Score down the middle and fold in half. Cut a piece of decorative backing paper 10 x 14.5cm (4 x 5¾in) and stick on the front of the folded card.

two Fit a metal nozzle to the pale gold paint applicator. Apply dots of pale gold along some edges of the patterned paper. Make the dots a reasonable size as they will shrink slightly as they dry.

three Apply dots of pale gold where you would like the sequins to be attached. Drop a peach sequin on each drop of paint and press down lightly. Apply a small dot of paint over the hole of each sequin.

four Fit a metal nozzle on the pink-gold paint applicator. Apply dots of paint on other parts of the design. Using a pin or fine tweezers, drop a pinky-lilac seed bead on every second paint dot. Leave to dry overnight.

trythis
Make a matching tag for a small gift. Cut a 6 x 10cm (2¼ x 4in) piece of backing paper with an interesting pattern and stick on to a piece of card the same size. Cut a circle from pink backing paper and stick on the tag so it overhangs the edge, then trim. Decorate the tag with paint dots, beads and sequins. Leave to dry overnight then punch a hole at the top and thread through a ribbon.

beads & felt

fab flowers album

Although it is often thought of as a cheap and cheerful craft product for children, felt can be used to make some stunning designs that would not look out of place in the most stylish homes. The secret is to choose your colours carefully, using toning colours to create a subtle effect. To make the cover, look out for bolts of felt that are often a slightly heavier weight, keeping the thinner felt squares for the motifs. Rather than trying to find lots of interesting individual beads, choose tubes of mixed beads in a colour to match the felt and then buy a few in a complementary colour for contrast. This album is about 18 x 25cm (7 x 10in).

right This pretty, floral design is ideal for a general photo album, but you could change the colours and make a wedding or baby album with letters and other simple motifs.

you will need...

- ✓ Paper and tracing paper
- ✓ Felt 30cm (12in) squares in mid blue, light blue and pale blue
- ✓ Fine black pen
- ✓ Cream felt 30 x 80cm (12 x 31½in)
- ✓ Translucent sequins 8mm (⁵⁄₁₆in)
- ✓ Selection of mixed small and medium blue beads

one Trace the template on page 112 and cut out paper patterns for the flowers and leaves. Pin the paper shapes on to the appropriate colour of felt and cut out. Cut the large piece of cream felt into two panels 30 x 40cm (12 x 16in).

quick & clever Because felt is quite thick, you can cover an old photo album or even buy a bargain in the sales to re-cover.

two Trace the template again with a fine black pen. Use a light box, or tape the paper template to a window and trace the outline of the oval wavy line on to the centre of one piece of cream felt. Thread three strands of brown linen thread on to a fine needle and sew running stitch along the line. Using the template as a guide, arrange the felt flowers around the stitched line and pin into position.

three Using a single length of pale blue sewing cotton, sew two sequins on to each petal of the large mid blue flowers. Using a double length of sewing thread, sew a large blue bead in the centre and surround it with a selection of medium beads, including bone beads to highlight. To secure the medium beads, bring a double thread up in the centre of the bead, pick up a seed bead and take the needle back through the larger bead and the felt (see also page 13 for sewing beads).

quick & clever When attaching beads it is best to secure the thread with two tiny backstitches rather than a knot, which could be pulled through the felt.

- ✓ Round bone beads 3mm (⅛in)
- ✓ Brown stranded linen thread
- ✓ Blue sewing thread
- ✓ Blue grosgrain ribbon 50cm (20in) of 7mm (¼in) wide
- ✓ Blue organza ribbon 50cm (20in) of 7mm (¼in) wide
- ✓ Photo album kit 25 x 17cm (10 x 6½in)
- ✓ Dressmaker's pins

four Create the centres of the small light blue flowers in the same way with different beads. Arrange the leaves between the flowers and stitch each in place with running stitch using three strands of linen thread. Fill in around the leaves with more mixed blue beads.

five Lay the felt on the front cover of the photo album, mark the size with pins and tack (baste) the outline. Trim the felt to 1.5cm (⅝in) outside the tacked line. Lay the felt face down and place the photo album cover on top.

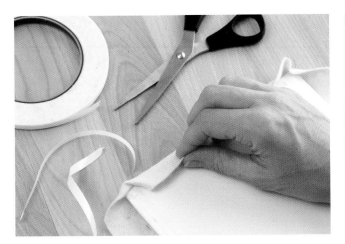

six Cut across the corners of the felt, about 6mm (¼in) away from the corners of the cover. Stick double-sided tape around the edge of the cover and peel off the backing paper. Tuck in the felt at each corner and then fold in the edges to make neat mitred corners. You can stitch invisibly with matching sewing thread to neaten.

seven Stick one of the inserts of the photo album on the inside to hide the raw edges. Cover the back cover with the remaining piece of cream felt and finish in the same way. Assemble the album with the leaves inside and sew a length of blue grosgrain and organza ribbons through the holes and tie in a bow. Trim the ends neatly to finish.

Piles of coloured felt squares in a craft shop look so enticing it's hard to resist buying a few every time you go in – but they'll be much more inspiring if you sort them into shades and tones or complementary colours. To embellish designs, use packs of mixed beads in colours that tone with your felt and you'll find the design almost creates itself.

natty needlecase

This sweet little bag has a hidden secret – it's really a needlecase. The needles are kept safe on a panel of felt inside. If sewing isn't your thing, make a small pocket on the inside flap of the felt booklet to turn the bag into a holder for a handbag mirror.

you will need...

✓ Paper and pencil
✓ 30cm (12in) squares of felt in pale blue and raspberry
✓ Stranded embroidery cotton (floss) in pink and blue
✓ Needles: sewing and large-eyed
✓ Assortment of blue seed beads
✓ Small star sequins in pink and blue
✓ Blue wax cotton thread

one Trace and cut out the template from page 114. From raspberry felt, cut the back panel with flap included. Fold down the flap on the template and cut two front pieces in pale blue felt.

two Sew an assortment of seed beads and star sequins along the bottom of one piece of the blue felt to make a narrow border, leaving about 1.25cm (½in) free along the bottom. Sandwich the plain piece of felt in the middle between the other two pieces so they line up and sew a line of running stitch along the bottom edge using three strands of pink embroidery cotton. If you have lots of needles to store, cut another panel of blue felt and layer with the others before sewing the bottom seam.

three Thread four large seed beads on to the wax cotton and tie a knot at either end. Add another five groups of beads along the length to make a handle. Sew the ends through the felt at the top of the flap and tie a knot on the inside.

four Attach a single group of beads to the point of the flap and tie off on the underside. Trim any long ends of wax cotton. Decorate the flap with running stitch in pink embroidery cotton and sew a few beads and sequins on the flap to finish. Store needles on the inside blue felt panel.

quick & clever To make a fastening, stick a pair of Velcro dots under the flap and sew into the felt.

fun felt box

Felt is the ideal material for covering a simple card box because it doesn't fray and motifs of any shape or size can be cut out. This bright box, decorated with shiny beads, is ideal for a young teenager, perhaps to store make-up.

quick & clever Don't try to draw the motif shape on to felt as the ink tends to sit on the surface and then come off on your hands – just pin on the template and cut out.

you will need...

✓ Card box 9cm (3½in) square

✓ 30cm (12in) squares of felt in fuchsia, pale blue and bright orange

✓ Stranded embroidery cotton (floss) in fuchsia

✓ Small quantity of bugle beads in fuchsia and pale blue

✓ Eight square beads 3mm (⅛in) each in fuchsia and pale blue

✓ Small quantity of seed beads in fuchsia and pale blue

one Cut two pieces of pale blue felt 11 x 9cm (3½ x 4½in) and two the same size from fuchsia. Lay two contrasting panels together and stitch a 6mm (¼in) seam using two strands of fuchsia embroidery thread. Stitch the other two panels together in the same way. Pin the panels around the box to check the fit, remove from the box, trim if required and stitch the other two seams.

two Trace the flower and flower centre from the template on page 113. Pin the flower and centre on to bright orange felt and cut out two of each shape. Cut out two fuchsia flowers and two pale blue flower centres.

three Pin the pale blue flower centres to the orange flowers and the orange centres to the fuchsia flowers. Sew a row of small running stitches around the centres to attach to the flower, using two strands of fuchsia or a contrast colour of stranded cotton.

four Secure two strands of pale blue cotton on the reverse side of a fuchsia flower. Bring the thread over between two petals, pick up a pale blue bugle and take the needle back through at the edge of the flower centre. Repeat all round the flower. Add square blue beads between each bugle.

five Embellish the orange flowers with fuchsia bugles and square beads in the same way. Stick the flowers on a contrast side of the box. Embellish the corners with some short lengths of bead fringing. To do this attach a thread in the corner, pick up alternate bugles and seed beads two or three times, add a square bead and another seed bead. Take the thread back up from the square bead and then make a second strand. Repeat on each corner. Slip the felt cover over the card box to finish.

beads & tigertail

Tigertail wire is ideal for jewellery as it doesn't kink or bend like ordinary wire; the beads sit elegantly on its soft sweeping curves.

plaited necklace

This unusual necklace is made from a range of contrasting materials that work together to create a stunning design. On the seven-strand tigertail are small washer-style beads and seed beads held in place with small crimp beads. There are also chunky beads threaded through a tubular wire-mesh ribbon spaced out with simple overhand knots. The organza ribbon weaves in and around the beaded strands to create a loosely plaited contemporary design. The weight of the necklace is kept to a minimum, because although they look quite authentic, these 'glass' beads are actually fashion beads made from lightweight plastic.

right Co-ordinating colours of beads, wire mesh and organza ribbons are combined to make this beautiful and unusual necklace. Choose an attractive gold-plated fastening to finish it off.

you will need...

✓ Seven-strand tigertail in gold, copper and olive, 200cm (80in) in total

✓ Gold-plated tubular crimps

✓ Mixed washer-style beads 6mm (¼in) in brown and copper

✓ Size 11 seed beads in brown and copper

✓ Larger beads in cream, pale yellow and light brown

one Take four 50cm (20in) lengths of tigertail in a range of toning colours and use masking tape to secure them in a bundle to the work surface. Pick up a crimp, a seed bead, a washer bead, a seed bead and a crimp. Push the beads and crimps along the tigertail to 5cm (2in) from the tape. Squeeze the top crimp with pliers and then push the second crimp tight against the beads and squeeze it too. Check the beads don't move.

two Pick up the same beads but in different shades, with crimps on either side on the same length of tigertail and secure about 8cm (3in) further down. Continue adding groups of beads stopping about 5cm (2in) from the end of the wire. On subsequent tigertail strands, move the beads down about 1.25cm (½in) so that they aren't level with any other beads.

three Tie the four different colours of organza ribbon together at one end. Lift the tigertail from the work surface and tie in a knot at one end. Pull the knot as tight as possible, and then trim the ends of the tigertail and organza ribbons close to the knots.

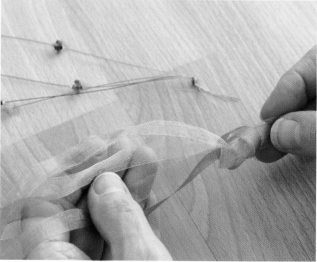

- ✓ Organza ribbon 50cm (20in) lengths of 9mm (⅜in) wide in four different colours
- ✓ Wire-mesh ribbon 60cm (24in) lengths in orange and copper
- ✓ Two gold-plated jump rings
- ✓ Two necklace crimp ends and a necklace fastening
- ✓ Masking tape
- ✓ Flat-nosed pliers and wire cutters

four Tie an overhand knot (see below) in one piece of the mesh ribbon about 5cm (2in) from one end. Feed a large bead inside the mesh up to the knot and tie a knot on the other side of the bead. Tie a knot about 4cm (1½in) further down and continue adding beads this way, stopping about 5cm (2in) from the end. Make a second mesh ribbon strand with beads in slightly different places along the length.

overhand knot

five Tie the wire-mesh ribbon strands together in a bundle, trim the ends and position with the tigertail and organza ribbon bundles within the crimp fastening. Squeeze the crimp together.

quick & clever Make a pair of matching earrings using an offcut of gold or copper tigertail, following the instructions on page 51.

six Tape the crimp fastening to the work surface and then loosely plait the strands together in a fairly haphazard way. Tie the groups of wires and ribbons together again at the other end and fit a second crimp fastening. Open a jump ring by holding it with two pairs of pliers and pushing the ends away from one another rather than pulling apart. Pick up the necklace fastening and the crimp fastening in the jump ring and close it again. Attach the other section of the necklace fastening on the other end to finish.

Tigertail is a bead threading material made from several strands of stainless steel wire, usually three or seven, and is coated with nylon so that it is more like a nylon thread than ordinary wire. It falls in gently sweeping curves that lend themselves beautifully to necklace design but will kink badly if bent. Commonly sold in silver and gold, you can get a whole range of exciting colours to inspire gorgeous designs.

thanks for the memory

This pretty little bracelet is made from another type of wire, memory wire, so-called because it bounces back into the same shape. You simply cut one or several spirals from the coil and add beads of your choice.

quick & clever You can buy special pliers for cutting memory wire because it is so hard, but for the occasional project use heavyweight wire cutters. Cut as far away from the tip of the pliers as possible, to give you more leverage.

you will need...

✓ A coil of bracelet memory wire

✓ Two silver-plated memory wire ball ends

✓ Superglue or strong jewellery glue

✓ Selection of beads in various shapes and sizes

✓ Memory wire cutters or heavyweight wire cutters

one To make this simple bracelet, coil the wire around your wrist to get the right size and then mark where you want to cut. Using memory wire cutters if you have them, cut the wire at the mark.

two Stick one of the memory wire ball ends on one end of the bracelet length using superglue or other strong glue.

three Pick up a selection of beads in toning colours and in a variety of shapes and sizes, leaving enough room to fit the second ball end. Trim the wire if necessary and then stick the ball end in place.

turquoise and lime duo

The brightly coloured seven-strand tigertail used for this project tones in with the beads beautifully and gives the finished necklace and earrings an almost luminous quality. Each strand has four of the same bead on it, but they look mixed up when the necklace is complete.

quick & clever Use tiny silver-plated or even sterling silver tubular crimps to hold the beads in place along the wires as their size is less intrusive than regular crimps.

you will need...

✓ Seven-strand lime tigertail 1.5m (60in)

✓ Seven-strand turquoise tigertail 1m (39in)

✓ Four blue/green leaf beads

✓ Four flat green beads 8mm (5⁄16in) diameter

✓ Four green beads 8mm (5⁄16in) diameter

✓ Four blue/green beads 8mm (5⁄16in) diameter

✓ Four turquoise beads 1.25cm (½in) diameter

✓ Small quantity of turquoise short bugle beads

✓ Small quantity of green seed beads

✓ Silver-plated crimp beads

✓ Silver-plated tigertail crimp necklace fastening

✓ Wire cutters and flat-nosed pliers

one Cut the tigertail into 50cm (20in) lengths and feed the ends of all five lengths into a crimp end of the necklace fastening. When all wires are pushed in far enough, squeeze the end of the fastening to secure.

two On one strand, pick up a crimp bead, a short bugle and a leaf bead. Add another short bugle and a crimp. Squeeze the first crimp about 8cm (3in) from the end, push the beads up tightly and then squeeze the second crimp to secure.

three Attach the remaining three leaf beads on the same strand, spacing the groups of beads every 6–7cm (2½–2¾in). On subsequent strands, add the first group a slightly different distance from the end and keep to the same large bead on each strand.

four Once all the beads are added, drape the tigertail strands attractively and cut the ends to the same length. Push the ends into the other end of the fastening and squeeze with pliers to secure as before.

try this

To make a matching pair of earrings, cut two 15cm (6in) lengths of seven-strand tigertail and loop each through a sterling silver earring wire. Feed on a 2mm (1⁄16in) silver-plated crimp and squeeze flat where the wires cross, close to the earring loop. Add a tubular crimp, seed bead, large bead, seed bead and crimp to each end and squeeze the crimps so that the beads lie about 3cm (1¼in) from the earring wire.

beads & polymer clay

Try this imaginative technique – embed beads into polymer clay to create unusual projects embellished with sparkling patterns.

polka dot box

Polymer clay is a wonderful material for making flat and three-dimensional craft projects. This funky little box is made in flat sections which are baked in a domestic oven to harden. The sides and base are then joined together using thin rolls of clay and re-baked to set. Polymer clay is generally matt but you can turn it into something really special by embellishing it with sparkling seed beads. If you use translucent clay for delicacy you can mix brightly coloured clay into it to create these fun translucent spots. The finished size of this box is a 7cm (2¾in) cube.

right This unusual little box is easy to make and suitable for various occasions. Why not make one in romantic colours for a valentine sweetheart and use a heart-shaped cutter?

you will need...

- ✓ Two large 50g (2oz) packs of translucent polymer clay
- ✓ Small packs 25g (1oz) of polymer clay in deep pink, bright green and bright blue
- ✓ Vegetable oil and kitchen paper towel
- ✓ Two ceramic tiles
- ✓ Two bamboo skewers

one Knead one pack of the translucent polymer clay until it is warm and has softened. Wipe a ceramic tile very lightly with a kitchen paper towel dipped in vegetable oil. Flatten the ball of translucent clay, position two bamboo skewers either side of the clay and roll out until the rolling pin touches the skewers.

quick & clever It's quite safe to embed seed beads into polymer clay before baking as they are made from glass and can be baked at the temperature required to harden the clay.

two To make one of the box sides, lay a 6cm (2⅜in) square of paper on the polymer clay and lightly mark the corners with a pin. Use a small round cutter or tube to cut five circles out of the clay. One or two of the circles can jut out of the square so only part of the circle is retained within the square shape. Use the point of a skewer to lift the circles out.

quick & clever You can use a non-stick baking sheet to roll out the clay and bake it on. Lift the baked clay off the tray and on to a flat surface to cool.

three Knead a small amount of deep pink clay into some translucent clay until it is completely mixed. Roll out the clay between bamboo skewers as before and cut out a few circles. Peel off the excess clay and lift the circles carefully with the edge of a knife. Make circles in blue and green clay in the same way. Fit the circles into the holes in the translucent clay and pat into position. Roll the clay lightly to seal the dots into the clay.

- ✓ Small rolling pin
- ✓ Sheet of plain paper
- ✓ Glass-headed pin
- ✓ 2.5cm (1in) diameter circular cutter
- ✓ Small knife
- ✓ Small quantities of seed beads in blue, lime and fuchsia
- ✓ Clay gun (optional)

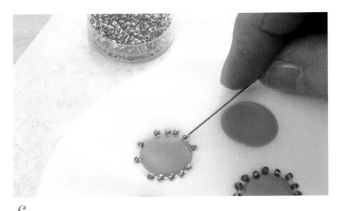

four Use a pin to position matching seed beads around each of the clay circles. To space the beads evenly, position the first four in quarters and then one halfway in between and so on. Press the beads gently with your fingers and then roll lightly.

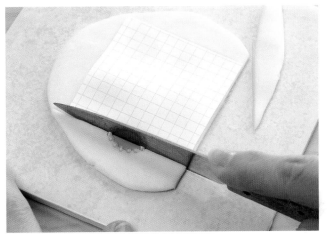

five Lay the square of paper used earlier on top of the dotty panel, cut along each side and lift away excess clay. Neaten the edges by patting lightly with the side of the knife. Leaving the panel on the tile, bake it in the oven at 130°C (250°F or gas mark ½) for no more than 20 minutes. Leave to cool and then lift off the tile. Make three more panels in the same way.

six To make the box base, roll out a ball of translucent clay to the thickness of the skewers. Use the template to mark the square on the clay. Press the panels along each side so they are level around the top. Trim excess clay. Mix a quantity of pink translucent clay and squeeze out a long thin roll using a clay gun. (Alternatively, roll out a sausage with your fingertips.) Gently press the roll down the edges and trim to length. Add another length around the bottom edge and join on one side. Bake as before.

seven Roll out more translucent clay for the lid. Cut out a circle and replace with a bright blue circle. Decorate with seed beads as before. Mix and roll a ball of pink and translucent clay and press gently on the dot. Make another length of thin pink roll with the clay gun and press around the edge of the lid. Bake as before and when cool, place the lid on the box to finish.

Polymer clay is available in a huge range of different colours as well as white, black, gold, silver and translucent. The clays can be mixed to create other shades to suit your beads. Press the beads into the clay or thread them on wire to string across an aperture.

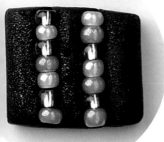

purple passion

Polymer clay is a super medium for making small embellishments for greetings cards. Simple shapes such as flowers and hearts are easiest to make. Embed the beads into the clay before baking and then add beads on wire to finish the design.

quick & clever Leave the polymer clay on the tile once it has been rolled and cut into shape and put the tile straight into the oven to bake.

you will need...

✓ Purple metallic polymer clay 25g (1oz)

✓ Lilac polymer clay 25g (1oz)

✓ Ceramic tile and rolling pin

✓ Vegetable oil and kitchen paper

✓ Vegetable knife

✓ Assorted seed beads in pink and purple

✓ Five washer-style beads

✓ Cream card 20cm (8in) square

✓ Sheet of decorative paper

✓ Paper-covered wire

✓ Strong glue such as Superglue

one Knead the purple metallic polymer clay for a minute or so until it is soft. Wipe a ceramic tile with a smear of vegetable oil. Roll the clay out to about 3mm (⅛in) thick. Trace the template from page 112 and use it to cut out a large and small flower shape from purple polymer clay. Mark the petals with a vegetable knife.

two Roll out the lilac clay in the same way and cut out a large flower. Lay the small purple flower on top and press gently to stick. Push a ceramic bead in each flower centre and pink seed beads at the end of each marked line on the petals.

Bake the pieces on a ceramic tile for 15–20 minutes at 130°C (250°F or gas mark ½). Lift out and leave to cool.

three Score and fold a 20cm (8in) square of cream card. Cut a strip of spotty paper 3 x 12cm (1¼ x 4¾in) and stick on the front of the card. Arrange the flowers on the card and cut two pieces of paper-covered wire to length. Feed on an assortment of seed beads, sticking them in place with Superglue. Use the glue to attach the wire to the back of the flowers. Stick the flowers and three washer-style ceramic beads on to the card to finish.

shooting star

A decorative key ring made from polymer clay is not ideal for keys that you carry around but is lovely for holding the keys of a conservatory or other interior door. During the day the key sits in the lock with its attractive beaded decoration and can be stored away at night.

quick & clever The deep pink beads on this key ring are actually made from polymer clay – just mark each ball with a dot so that it looks realistic.

you will need...

- ✓ Bright pink polymer clay 25g (1oz)
- ✓ Deep pink polymer clay 25g (1oz)
- ✓ Ceramic tile and rolling pin
- ✓ Vegetable oil and kitchen paper
- ✓ Vegetable knife
- ✓ Cocktail stick and pin
- ✓ Gold beads 2mm (1/16in)
- ✓ Gold seed beads
- ✓ Wooden bead 9mm (7/8in)
- ✓ Short length of gold tigertail
- ✓ Gold machine embroidery thread
- ✓ Two gold crimps
- ✓ Wire cutters and flat-nosed pliers
- ✓ Key ring fitment and triangle bail fastening

one Trace the template from page 113 and cut out. Wipe a ceramic tile with a smear of vegetable oil. Roll the bright pink polymer clay out on the tile to about 3mm (1/8in) thick. Lay the template on top and cut along the edges with a vegetable knife. Peel off excess clay.

two Make a hole at a V shape on the star using a cocktail stick. At each of the other V shapes drop a 2mm (1/16in) gold bead off the end of a pin and press into the clay. Push tiny gold seed beads in a ring inside the larger beads and then add two down each side of all points of the star so that all the holes face up.

three Roll out a thin sausage in deep pink clay and cut tiny pieces off this. Roll each piece into a ball, making 32 in varying sizes. Press the balls between the tiny gold beads on the points of the stars. Mark each ball with a cocktail stick to make a 'bead' hole. Roll a larger bead in deep pink and one in bright pink and push a cocktail stick through each to make a hole. Bake all pieces on the tile at 130°C (250°F or gas mark ½) for 15–20 minutes.

four To make the head of the tassel, tie a gold thread through the hole in the wood bead and pick up about 10 seed beads. Take the thread through the hole so the beads lie in a line down the bead. Keep adding rows of beads to cover the wood bead. Add fewer beads towards the end to cover the bead entirely.

five Wrap the gold thread around four fingers to make a small bundle and cut at one side. Loop the tigertail under the thread bundle and take the ends through the tassel head. Pick up the two polymer clay beads and a crimp bead. Squeeze the crimp with flat-nosed pliers to secure and cut off one end only. Pick up about 15 gold seed beads and a crimp bead on the remaining wire, fold over at the end to form a small loop and feed back through the crimp and beads. Squeeze the crimp to secure.

six Attach the key ring fitment to the star with a triangle bail fastening, or simply bend wire into a triangle shape with the join on the short side. Feed the loop of the tassel on to the key ring to finish.

bead jewellery

charm bracelet

Once you realize how easy it is to make a bead charm using a silver- or gold-plated head pin you will never be out of jewellery to match an outfit or any occasion. A head pin is rather like a very large dressmaker's pin. They can be of varying lengths but remember that it is always easier to bend a long pin rather than a short one. To make this attractive charm bracelet you can add beads to a ready-made bracelet or add bracelet fastenings to a length of silver- or gold-plated chain.

right When making a charm bracelet choose a variety of beads in a range of sizes and shapes and attach the beads so that they all hang from the same side of the chain.

you will need...

- ✓ Silver-plated chunky chain bracelet
- ✓ Selection of pink, white and turquoise beads
- ✓ Crystal bugles 30mm (1¼in)

- ✓ Silver-plated wire 0.6mm (24 gauge)
- ✓ Silver-plated jump rings
- ✓ Silver-plated head pins
- ✓ Round-nosed pliers, flat-nosed pliers and wire cutters

one Open out the chain bracelet and lay out the beads along the length to achieve an attractive balance of shapes, colours and sizes. Use long beads such as bugles to create depth or position several beads on top of one another.

quick & clever If you don't have a plain chain bracelet simply buy a length of chain from the bead shop and attach bracelet fastenings at each end.

two Make the beads into charms using head pins or wire. If the bead has a small enough hole, simply thread it on to a head pin. Using round-nosed pliers, hold the head pin close to the bead and wind the wire around once or twice. Trim the wire end close to the loop and then hold the loop in the round-nosed pliers and bend back slightly to straighten.

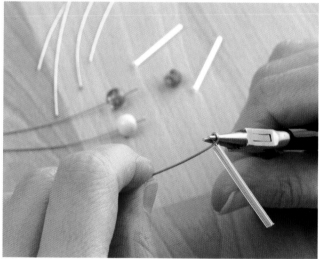

three If you like, you can pick up several beads on the head pin to make a longer charm before making a ring at the top end as before. If the bead hole is slightly larger than the head pin, pick up a seed bead before the larger bead so that it doesn't come off the end. Make a ring at the top as before.

four Beads with larger holes can be attached using silver-plated wire. Cut a short length of wire and place the bead in the middle. Fold the wire in half and twist the two ends together for 5–7mm (³⁄₁₆–¼in).

five Wind one end of the wire around the round-nosed pliers twice to form a loop. Carefully cut off the ends of the wire close to the ring.

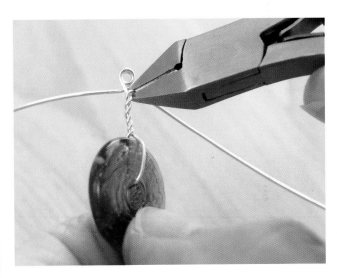

quick & clever To open a jump ring, hold it on either side of the join with two pairs of pliers. Push the ends away from one another to open them. Once the charm is attached reverse the process to close.

six Lay the bracelet out so the chain is not twisted. Lay out the beads along the length. Open the jump rings one at a time and attach the charms. The beads should be attached on the same side of the chain so that they hang in the right way.

Bead shops are often rather like Aladdin's cave, with beads seeming to spill from boxes on every possible surface. They always look so inspiring because they are usually arranged by colour and as you zoom in on your favourite colour scheme the choice can be almost overwhelming. While you are there do invest in a set of jewellery tools, which will make your task much easier – a pair of round-nosed pliers, flat-nosed pliers and wire cutters are all you need to begin.

kilt pin

Using a small piece of jewellery to create a greetings card is the ideal way to tell someone they are really special. The kilt pin used for this project is specially designed for adding beads with a row of little rings along the lower bar.

quick & clever The kilt pin can be used as an accessory on a bag, cardigan or coat – it's so pretty you won't want to give it away.

you will need...

✓ A kilt pin
✓ Assortment of medium-sized beads in pink
✓ Silver-plated head pins
✓ Jump rings
✓ Round-nosed pliers, flat-nosed pliers and wire cutters
✓ Silver-plated wire 0.6mm (24 gauge)
✓ Fine silver-plated chain
✓ White single-fold card
✓ Pink ribbon to trim
✓ Pink ink stamp pad or pink paint

one Choose a selection of beads of different shapes and sizes to make the kilt pin decoration. Make each bead into a charm using a silver-plated head pin or wire. The method used depends on the style of the bead – see the charm bracelet instructions on page 60 to help you decide.

two Attach the charms to the kilt pin with silver-plated jump rings. To add depth to the design, cut two short lengths of silver-plated chain and attach these to the kilt pin with jump rings too.

three Colour the edge of a plain white card with a pink ink stamp pad (or sponge on pink paint). Cut a length of pink ribbon and fold over the top bar of the kilt pin. Tape the ribbon on the reverse side of the card and cover the raw edges with a white label or matching piece of card.

luscious links

The wire technique used to make this necklace is so versatile that once you know how to make the simple link you will be able to make matching bracelets and earrings too.

quick & clever Look out for tubes of mixed beads in toning colours – it saves agonizing over which individual beads to buy.

quick & clever Use 0.6mm (24 gauge) wire to make this necklace. It is just the right weight to hold the shape of the links but still looks delicate.

you will need...

✓ Silver-plated wire 0.6mm (24 gauge)
✓ Selection of mixed pink beads
✓ Selection of mixed pink seed beads
✓ Seven silver-plated head pins
✓ Seven silver-plated jump rings
✓ Round-nosed pliers, flat-nosed pliers and wire cutters

one Cut 15cm (6in) of the silver-plated wire. Hold the wire in the round-nosed pliers so it is about 6mm (¼in) down from the tips of the pliers and you can just feel the end of the wire jutting out between the blades. Bend the wire around the blades using your thumb until it is flat on the other side. Now take the wire off the pliers and bend the tail back slightly to straighten.

two Pick up beads to make the link, for example: 3 seed beads, a larger bead and another 3 seed beads. To make the ring at the other end of the beads, hold the wire so that there is a wire's width gap between the beads and the pliers. Make sure the wire is 6mm (¼in) from the tips of the pliers again.

three Bend the wire around the pliers to form a ring at the other end and, with the tips of the wire cutters, snip the tail of the wire off exactly where the wires cross over. Bend the ring slightly to straighten. Hold both rings between finger and thumb, and twist until the rings are level. This is the basic bead link – now simply make enough links to go around your neck and join them all together.

four To open the links, hold the ring at one end in flat-nosed pliers and bend up slightly to open. Join a second link on and then bend the ring down again to close. Attach a necklace fastening to each end.

five To make the drop attachment at the bottom of the necklace open the jump rings then join them all together in a chain. Attach the end one to the centre link of the necklace. Make seven bead charms using the head pins (see bracelet page 60) and attach one to each ring.

try this ....
Make matching earrings with one basic link and a bead charm, attached to earring wires. Complete your jewellery set with a bracelet using the same links.

beaded motifs

Beaded motifs are a quick and easy way to add instant glamour to all sorts of items. Some you don't need to sew – just iron on the reverse.

sequin flower bag

A little shoulder bag is so useful when going out to an evening party as it leaves your hands free for holding a glass of wine and you can still pick up the party nibbles! As with all sewing projects, the quality of the fabric determines the finished result. You only need a small quantity so choose something really opulent, such as a gorgeous silk dupion or taffeta. Make sure the fabric is firm enough to support the weight of the motifs – if in doubt iron some lightweight interfacing on the reverse side of the fabric before making up. The bag shown is 18 x 14cm (7 x 5½in), excluding strap.

right For evening, use a gorgeous silk dupion but if you are simply making a little day bag for a teenager you could use a pretty cotton poplin or linen fabric.

beaded motifs

you will need...

- ✓ Sheet of white paper
- ✓ Purple silk dupion 23 x 80cm (9 x 31½in)
- ✓ Burgundy silk dupion 35cm (14in) square
- ✓ Two matching iron-on sequin flower motifs
- ✓ Sequins to tone with fabrics
- ✓ Matching sewing thread

quick & clever If you don't have time to make a bag use sparkly sequin motifs singly or in pairs to decorate a ready-made bag.

quick & clever The shape of the flap for this bag was designed to fit these particular motifs; if you would prefer a straight or even curved flap simply draw a different flap shape at step 1.

one Draw a 28 x 14cm (11 x 5½in) rectangle for the back bag panel. To create the flap, measure 7cm (2¾in) down from the top edge on both sides and join with a dotted line. Draw a diagonal line from the dotted line on the left-hand side to the top-right corner. For the front bag panel, draw a rectangle 18 x 14cm (7 x 5½in). Cut out both pattern pieces.

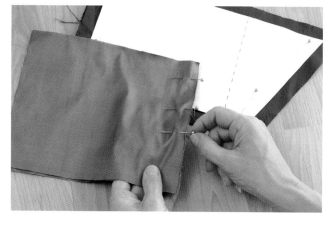

two Pin the larger pattern piece on to a double layer of burgundy silk dupion and the smaller pattern piece to a double layer of purple silk dupion. Cut out with 1.5cm (⅝in) seam allowances all round. Pin the two rectangles together with right sides facing and machine stitch along one short edge. Trim to 6mm (¼in), press open and fold so the seam is on the inside.

three Snip into the dotted line marked on the pattern piece on the two burgundy silk pieces. Machine stitch from the snip, around the diagonal flap down to the snip on the other side. Trim the seam around the flap to 6mm (¼in) and trim across the point. Turn the flap through, ease out the point and press.

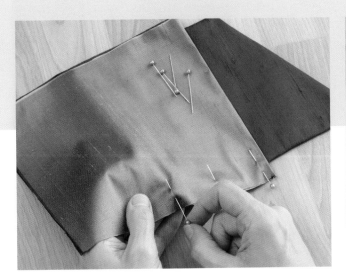

four Pin the front bag panel to the flap panel so that the front panel is level with the snips in the side seams of the back bag panel. Stitch the side and bottom seams. Zigzag the seams and trim close to the stitching. Trim across the corners, turn through, ease out the corners and press.

five To make the strap, cut a 3.5 x 80cm (1⅜ x 31½in) length of purple silk. Fold in half lengthways and sew the length with a 6mm (¼in) seam allowance. Tie the thread ends to a bodkin and feed back through the strap, easing the fabric along the thread to turn the strap through to the right side. Press with the seam at one side.

quick & clever The flower motifs used here were originally all one colour but made more interesting by swapping the centre sections in the flowers.

six Using matching sewing thread, sew sequins on one side of the strap every 2cm (¾in) along the length. Fold over the cut ends and pin to the back of the bag just below the flap fold line. Machine stitch a rectangle shape at each end of the strap to secure.

seven Position the motifs on the flap of the bag so that the edge of the flap is along the middle of the motifs (see picture on page 65). Iron the flap from the reverse side to secure the motifs (or sew in place if your bead motifs aren't the iron-on type). Sew a few sequins on the flap around the motifs to finish.

Beaded motifs come in all shapes and sizes – from tiny hearts to giant butterflies They can be decorated with beads or sequins or even a combination of the two. Use them to add instant glamour and sparkle and remember they're not just for evening – there is a bead motif suitable for everyone and every occasion.

bead bouquet

Beaded motifs often inspire the design, and that is certainly how this greetings card came about. The little flower motifs were shuffled about on the card until the idea of creating a little bouquet came to mind.

quick & clever Make a matching tag with a single beaded flower motif and attach to your gift with some sheer pink ribbon.

you will need...

✓ Three sequin flower motifs 3.5cm (1½in) in toning colours

✓ Narrow satin ribbon three 13cm (5in) lengths

✓ Pink single-fold card 9 x 19cm (3½ x 7½in)

✓ Sheer pink ribbon 0.5m (½yd) of 2.5cm (1in) wide

✓ Dry adhesive tape

✓ Craft glue dots or Superglue

one Arrange the three sequin flower motifs on the card and with a pencil mark the bottom edge where the 'stems' will begin.

two Stick the lengths of narrow ribbon on to the dry adhesive tape and peel off again. Stick the top raw edge of the middle ribbon over the pencil mark. Gently curve the ribbon as you stick it down on the card.

Attach the other ribbons so that they cross over the centre stem about 8cm (3in) from the bottom of the card.

three Tie the sheer ribbon in a large bow and stick where the ribbons cross over. Trim the ends at an angle near the bottom of the card. Stick the sequin flowers in position using a craft glue dot or Superglue.

flutterby diary

Didn't you just love the lockable 5-year diary that you had as a child? This gorgeous beaded diary is the adult equivalent and much more stylish! Instead of a lock the diary is secured by wrapping organza ribbon round and round.

quick & clever Buy a pretty, ready-made diary in suede, handmade paper or fabric and embellish it with a few bead motifs – you can still add the ribbons, just stick the flyleaf down to secure the diary.

you will need...

- ✓ Two sequin butterfly motifs 6 x 4cm (2⅜ x 1½in)
- ✓ Two sequin butterfly motifs 3 x 2.5cm (1¼ x 1in)
- ✓ Diary or notebook A5 size 21 x 14.5cm (8¼ x 5¾in)
- ✓ Thin wadding (batting) 21 x 32cm (8¼ x 12½in)
- ✓ Silk dupion 30 x 38cm (12 x 15in)
- ✓ Organza ribbon 71cm (28in) lengths in pink and cream
- ✓ Double-sided tape

one Stick the wadding (batting) over the outside of the diary using double-sided tape and trim neatly to the exact size of your book.

two Lay the open diary on the reverse side of the silk so that there is an equal border all round. Stick double-sided tape around one inside cover. Snip into the fabric at both sides of the spine.

three Fold the two corners over and then fold in the side edges to make neat mitred corners. Repeat on the other cover, but check that the book will close after you fold in the corners and adjust before you finish the mitred corners.

four Stick one piece of organza ribbon in the centre on the inside of the front cover and the other inside the back cover. Stick double-sided tape around the edge of the flyleaf and stick it down to cover the raw edges of fabric.

five Tie the ribbon around the diary and then stick the larger butterfly motifs on the cover using double-sided tape or craft glue dots. Stick the small butterfly motifs on the end of the ribbons and neaten the backs of the motifs with pieces of card cut to the same size.

accent beads

Accent beads, which are like tiny ball bearings, are used with seed beads and bugles to create an encrusted, sparkly effect.

cool christmas trees

Although the decorations are packed away carefully every year ready to be brought out again the following Christmas, it is always a good idea to make something new from time to time. These beautiful cone-shaped decorations are simple to make and will last for years if wrapped in tissue paper and stored away carefully. The simple beading technique can be used to cover different shapes as long as the hi-tack tape will wrap around fairly neatly. Narrow tape works better on shaped sides than wider tape but you may need to experiment.

These trees are 21cm (8¼in) tall.

right A beaded tree decoration is not just for Christmas! Use non-traditional colours like silver and blue and you'll be able to bring them out for special occasions too.

you will need... (for one tree)

✓ Oasis or polystyrene cone shape
✓ Hi-tack tape 5mm (¼in) wide and hi-tack film

✓ Seed beads in light blue
✓ Bugles in dark blue
✓ Medium silver accent beads
✓ Tiny silver accent beads

one Beginning at the bottom of the cone, stick the hi-tack tape at a slight angle and begin to wind the tape around the cone, so that when it comes round to the same side again there will be a 6mm (¼in) gap between the two bands of tape.

two Continue wrapping the tape around the cone until you reach the top and then trim neatly. Begin at the bottom edge again with a second band of tape, filling in the gap carefully. Make sure that the tip of the cone is completely covered with tape this time.

three Pour a mix of seed beads and bugles into a tray. Peel off just one of the strips of tape from around the cone. Lay the cone in the tray and press into the beads. Roll it around and press the beads on to the tape. You may have to lift beads up and press them on with your fingers. Don't worry if it's not completely covered as the gaps will be filled later.

✓ Small glass nightlight holder
✓ Small tray
✓ Polythene bag (sandwich bag)

four Carefully peel off the second band of tape. Work over a tray or sheet of newspaper, as some of the beads are bound to pop off. Change the beads in the tray to a quantity of medium silver accent beads. Roll the cone around as before until it is covered as much as possible. Shake off any excess beads.

five Pour the finer silver accent beads into a large polythene bag. Put the cone in the bag and shake about until all the tiny gaps are filled. You can use the bag at this stage, as the hi-tack tape has been covered with beads.

six Draw around the base of the cone on to the backing paper of hi-tack film and cut out. Peel off the backing paper and stick on the base of the cone. You can stick a small glass nightlight holder to the base at this stage to make the tree 'trunk'. To finish, put the whole decoration back in the fine accent beads bag to cover the exposed hi-tack film.

quick & clever A small glass nightlight holder makes a good tree trunk and also adds weight so the decoration doesn't fall over.

Accent beads are tiny no-hole beads that are attached with glue or strong sticky tape rather than by sewing. They can be used to decorate all sorts of things, from greetings cards to gifts and ornaments. Cut or punch motifs from hi-tack film or create borders and bands with tape. You can also paint or draw shapes with strong PVA glue and dip in beads to create instant sparkly motifs.

in the spotlight

The sheet version of tacky tape is ideal for attaching accent and other small beads to large flat areas such as a picture frame. You can punch shapes such as circles, flowers or hearts to decorate with contrasting beads.

quick & clever Punch circles out of hi-tack film. Stick these directly on to a ready-made frame and then dip into accent beads to create pretty, beaded spots.

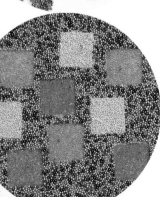

you will need...

✓ Medium red accent beads
✓ Small red accent beads
✓ Small gold accent beads
✓ Mixed gold, red and orange bugles and seed beads
✓ Small square picture frame
✓ Hi-tack film
✓ Small tray

one Lay a sheet of paper over one side of your frame and cut a pattern with angled corners to cover the front and side surfaces. Now use the pattern to cut four pieces of hi-tack film. Peel off the backing paper and stick on to the frame.

two Cut or punch four large circles and four small circles from hi-tack film. Lay the large circles on the frame so that they overlap the edge and crease to mark where to cut. Peel off the top layer of backing paper from the frame. Cut the large circles, peel off the backing paper and stick on the frame. Punch smaller circles and stick in the gaps in between.

three Pour the medium red accent beads into a small tray and shake the frame about in the beads to cover the background. Change the beads in the tray to the fine red accent beads and repeat the process. Shake off excess beads.

four Peel off the top layer of backing paper from all circles and dip the frame in the seed bead/bugle bead mix, pressing the beads on to the circles. Pour small gold accent beads over the circles to fill any remaining gaps and then tip off the excess.

close to my heart

Use a ready-made card to make this romantic heart card with pretty pink accent beads and matching buttons. If you can't find this type of card, cut small square apertures instead to make a similar design.

quick & clever If you are short of time cut heart shapes from hi-tack to decorate a plain card, and embellish with beads.

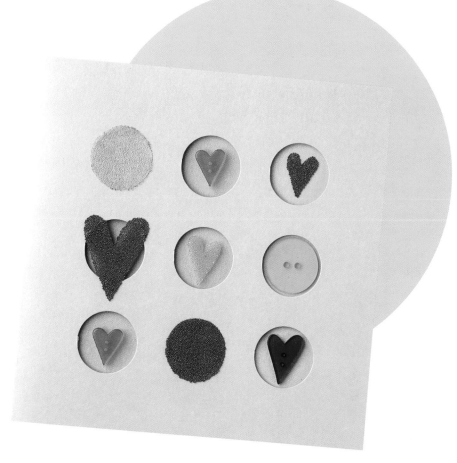

you will need...

✓ Single-fold card 15cm (6in) square with nine circles, in pearlescent pink

✓ Red and pink accent beads

✓ A4 (US letter) sheet of acetate

✓ Hi-tack film

✓ Three red translucent heart buttons

✓ Pink button 2cm (⅞in)

one Use a craft knife to trim the part-cut circles from their apertures. Cut a panel of acetate to cover the six circles on the left-hand side of the card and stick on the inside of the card.

two Cut hi-tack film to fit two of the apertures and peel off the backing. Sprinkle pink accent beads on one and red beads on the other. Stick the pink accent bead circle on the top left circular aperture and the red accent bead circle on the bottom middle circular aperture.

three Draw two small hearts and a large heart on the hi-tack film. Cut out and peel off the top paper. Sprinkle pink accent beads on one small heart and red accent beads on the other two hearts.

four Peel the backing paper from the hearts. Stick the large red heart on the centre left aperture, the pink one in the centre aperture and the small heart in the middle of the aperture on the top right. (This will actually be stuck on the inside of the card.) Stick the three heart buttons in the remaining apertures to finish.

try this

Make a matching tag using similar techniques. Cut a rectangle of red card and punch or cut a large circle at one end. Punch a small hole at the other end. Draw a heart on the hi-tack film and cut out. Peel off the white backing paper and dip in pink accent beads. Stick the heart across the circle aperture.

beads & fabric

Fabric can be embellished with just a few beads to create a really luxurious look – use the fabric pattern to inspire the beading design.

flower cluster box

Simple papier mâché or card boxes can be easily transformed into an exquisite beaded box suitable for jewellery or knick-knacks, which would make a lovely gift for a special friend. You can buy satin-covered boxes with a padded lid insert that can be covered with beaded fabric – these are often sold for cross stitch designs. Alternatively use an ordinary box and stretch the fabric over layers of wadding (batting) as shown here, and then finish with ribbon. If you can't find a box in the right colour it is quite easy to cover the box with mulberry paper to match the beaded fabric. The box shown is 11.5cm (4½in) in diameter.

right Choose beads that tone in with the pattern of the fabric, so that they look like they belong, then create texture with a variety of bead sizes and shapes.

you will need...

- ✓ Floral print fabric 25cm (10in) square
- ✓ Lightweight iron-on interfacing 25cm (10in) square

- ✓ Assortment of beads including seed beads, bugles and larger beads
- ✓ Gift box 11.5cm (4½in) diameter
- ✓ Thin wadding (batting) 12 x 36cm (4¾ x 14in)

one Choose an area of your fabric that has an attractive pattern. Cut it out at least 5cm (2in) larger all round and iron a similar-sized piece of interfacing on the reverse side. Lay the fabric on the carpet or other soft surface and press the lid into the fabric to make an indented mark. Tack (baste) around the marked line.

two Using sewing thread to match the beads, thread a needle with a double length and secure on the reverse side of the fabric with a couple of backstitches. Bring the needle to the right side where you want the first bugle, pick up a bugle, lay it flat and take the needle back through at the end of the bead. Stitch further beads around the petals in a slightly irregular way (see also page 13 for sewing on beads).

three Create the centre of the flowers using the larger round beads. Bring the needle with a double thread up in the centre of the flower, pick up a large round bead and then a seed bead. Take the needle back through the large bead and fabric. Add several more large beads and then fill in with smaller beads, simply sewing through the bead and back into the fabric.

- ✓ Double-sided tape
- ✓ Thin card
- ✓ Grosgrain ribbon 40cm (16in) to tone with fabric
- ✓ Fabric embroidery marker

four To extend the beads further over the fabric, create a few beaded fronds between the petals. Draw frond lines with an embroidery marker. Bring the double thread out between two petals and pick up 3–5 seed beads. Put the needle back in the fabric at the end of the beads and take a backstitch along the line, back 2 or 3 beads. Pull the needle and thread through and feed the needle back through the beads again. Continue adding beads in this way to make the fronds.

five For extra dimension, add three or four spikes to each flower centre. To make a spike, bring the needle and double thread out between larger beads. Pick up 5 seed beads, a large round bead and another seed bead. Miss the seed bead just added and take the needle back through the other beads and fabric.

quick & clever If the beaded fabric is lightweight stretch a piece of Swiss organza or other firm, fine fabric over the wadding before covering with the beaded fabric.

six Stick 1.25cm (½in) wide double-sided tape around the rim of the lid. Cut three pieces of thin wadding (batting) the same size as the box lid. Use double-sided tape to stick the bottom piece on to the lid.

seven Position the beaded fabric over the wadding and stretch down on to the rim of the box lid. Use the tacked line as a guide for how far to stretch and try to keep the fabric as flat as possible. Trim the fabric neatly just above the bottom edge of the lid. Remove tacking. Cut a strip of thin card to fit around the rim and stick in place. To finish, stick the grosgrain ribbon over the card; trim neatly where the ribbon overlaps and stick down.

All sorts of fabric can be embellished with beads or sequins to make it more decorative or opulent. Fabrics with a bold pattern or motif are easy to bead as you can use the design for inspiration – simply sew beads into the design to enhance the pattern, as I did for the little box on the previous page. To bead on plain fabrics, create your own motifs and transfer the design on to the fabric before beginning.

starry nights

Turn plain little gift bags into something really special with a few well-placed sequins. Sequins are ideal for gift bags as they are flat, come in all sorts of shapes and sizes and in a wide range of lovely colours.

quick & clever Look out for ready-made organza gift bags in your local gift shop. They are sold in a variety of colours and sizes and will save you time.

you will need...

✓ Organza fabric 14 x 46cm (5½ x 18in)

✓ Fine cord 75cm (30in)

✓ Thirteen silver star sequins 1.5mm (⅝in)

✓ Twelve silver sequins 6mm (¼in)

✓ Fine silver embroidery thread

✓ Dry adhesive tape or fabric glue

✓ Needle and bodkin

one To make the bag, fold the organza in half widthways and stitch the side seams. Trim seams to 6mm (¼in) and turn through. Fold down the top edge by 6cm (2⅜in) and machine stitch a 1.25cm (½in) casing 4cm (1½in) down from the top edge.

two Snip into the side seams between the casing lines. Cut the cord in half and, using a bodkin, thread one piece through from one side and back out the same gap. Thread the other end through from the other side. Knot the ends together.

three Stick the star sequins and round sequins in rows across the organza bag. Use a tiny dot of fabric glue (not near the hole in the sequin) or use a dry adhesive tape. If you use wet glue to stick the sequins, tuck baking parchment inside the bag to prevent the fabric layers sticking together. Sew a line of running stitch along in rows, backstitching through the holes of the sequins to secure. Sew in the ends on the reverse side to finish.

heart's desire

A hook fastening is ideal for making key rings, and because it opens on a spring on one side it can also be attached as an embellishment to a belt, trouser loop or even a bag.

quick & clever If you don't have scraps of velvet and organza, buy short lengths of wide velvet and sheer ribbons instead to make the heart embellishment.

you will need...

- ✓ Scraps of dark blue velvet, dark blue organza and metallic blue organza
- ✓ Rainbow metallic and dark blue machine embroidery threads
- ✓ Mixed denim blue beads
- ✓ Head pins 8cm (3in) long
- ✓ Short lengths of silver-plated chain
- ✓ Silver-plated wire 0.6mm (24 gauge)
- ✓ Swivel-hook fastening
- ✓ Round-nosed pliers

one Lay the dark blue organza over a piece of velvet. Cut a 3cm (1¼in) wide strip of metallic organza and pin on top. Trace the heart from page 113 and cut out. Pin the heart on the fabrics and tack (baste) around the edge to hold the layers together and mark the shape.

two Using rainbow metallic embroidery thread in your sewing machine and a darning or free-style embroidery foot, sew a swirling pattern inside the heart. Change the thread to dark blue and repeat a similar pattern on top.

quick & clever You can simply stitch a swirly pattern inside the heart outline using backstitch if you don't want to embroider by machine.

three Cut two heart shapes smaller than the original template in velvet for padding and lay on the reverse side inside the tacking lines. Lay a larger heart of velvet on top. Tack through all layers again. Machine stitch in a narrow satin stitch in dark blue around the tacking line. Trim the excess fabric and then zigzag again over the previous stitching.

four Cut a short length of silver-plated chain and sew it to the top of the heart. Now fit a large jump ring (see quick & clever below) to the other end and fit on to the hook fastening.

quick & clever To make large jump rings, bend one of the head pins around a knitting needle or rod to make a tight coil. Use wire cutters to snip on one side of each coil to separate into rings.

five Pick up a few mixed denim beads on a head pin and use round-nosed pliers to make a ring at the end (see page 60). Make another with slightly different beads. Pick up about 3cm (1¼in) of beads on two head pins. Make a ring at the end and trim off excess wire. Attach one of the short head pins to a short length of silver-plated wire. Fit all the embellishments to the hook fastening.

beads & paper

There is a wealth of gorgeous papers in a wide range of colours and textures just calling out to be embellished with all sorts of beads.

journal au naturel

If you are one of those people who tend to write things on scraps of paper and post-it notes and then can't find the information when you need it then this journal is for you. Inside the beautiful cover is a simple spiral-bound notebook, which could be used for keeping those notes and bits of information all in one place. The paper you choose to cover the journal should be fairly strong but more decorative papers can be applied and embellished with a selection of beads and sequins. Don't worry if you don't have a sewing machine – the journal will look just as good if hand stitched.

right Natural beads such as coco, wood and ceramic work beautifully with handmade paper. Choose colours of beads and papers that match for a harmonious look.

you will need...

✓ Spiral-bound notebook 12.5 x 14.5cm (5 x 5¾in)

✓ A3 sheet of stiff card

✓ Assorted coloured handmade papers in peach, soft brown and blue/green

✓ A3 sheet of heavy off-white handmade paper

✓ Turquoise seed beads

quick & clever Make a bead and paper cover to turn an address book or diary into something really special.

one Open out the notebook and lay it on top of the off-white paper. Mark the size of the book lightly with a pencil and cut out 5cm (2in) outside the edge all round. Tear narrow strips of coloured paper to extend outside the marked area and position on what will be the front of the book. Stitch the paper in place using contrast threads. Stitch without thread to create some interesting textured lines between the papers.

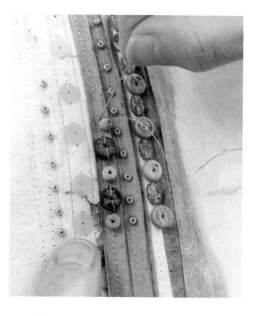

two Hand stitch beads down some of the stitched lines using gold thread. To keep washer-style beads flat, bring the needle up in the centre of the bead and take a stitch over one side. Bring the needle back through the hole and over the opposite side. Attach sequins and seed beads in the same way until happy with the arrangement.

quick & clever To work out the size of backing card for a different notebook, open out the book and lay it on the card. Mark 6mm (¼in) above and below it and 2.5cm (1in) out from both ends.

three For this particular size of notebook, cut a 31.5 x 16cm (12½ x 6¼in) piece of stiff card. Mark the centre at the top and bottom of the card and then every 6mm (¼in) out for 1.5cm (⅝in) on both sides. Score between the marks using an embossing tool or bone folder and then shape the spine by bending along the score lines.

- ✓ Assortment of natural wood and glass beads, including washer-style beads
- ✓ Sewing thread in peach and blue/green
- ✓ Double-sided tape 2.5cm (1in) wide
- ✓ Fine jute string
- ✓ Embossing tool or bone folder

four
Cut the beaded paper panel 1.5cm (⅝in) outside the pencil lines and rub out the pencil lines. Put two or three bands of double-sided tape down the inside of the paper panel and remove the backing tape.

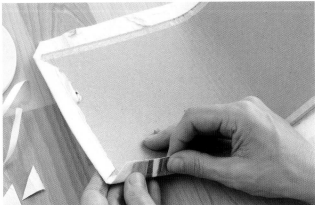

five
Stick the stiff card in place and trim across the first two corners leaving about 3mm (⅛in) of paper sticking out. Fold in one short edge first and tuck in the 3mm (⅛in) with a bone folder and then fold in the long edge and mitre the corners neatly. Check that the new cover and notebook will close before cutting across the other corners and completing the cover.

six
Remove the outer covers of the notebook and stick double-sided tape around the edges of the outside leaves of paper. Open the notebook and position it in the centre of the stiff card. Cut two lengths of jute string. Stick the end of the string down and fold it back on itself. Cut pieces of paper or thin card about 14 x 15cm (5½ x 6in) to cover the inside and stick in place.

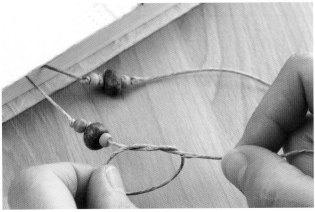

seven
Loop a double length of jute string through the top coil on the notebook and tuck inside the notebook with the ends sticking out underneath. Tie a knot in each string, thread on a bead, tie a knot and then repeat with larger beads. Add a small bead if required and then knot. Trim the ends neatly to finish.

Paper is one of the most versatile craft mediums and because of its tactile qualities is especially effective when paired with beads. There are all sorts of papers, from the finest tissue paper to heavyweight card, which can be used to create beautiful projects. To get the best effect choose beads that have similar qualities to the paper – natural beads with handmade papers and glossy beads with shiny paper.

pyramid posy

In next to no time make a simple but effective gift box that requires no awkward folding. Choose your favourite colour of card and select sequins and beads to match.

you will need...

- ✓ A3 sheet of mottled blue card
- ✓ Mixed flower sequins 9mm (⅜in), including white, blue and turquoise
- ✓ Clear rainbow sequins 4mm (³⁄₁₆in)
- ✓ Crystal seed beads and bugle beads
- ✓ Blue metallic thread
- ✓ Organza ribbon 1.25cm (½in) wide for a bow
- ✓ Clear-drying glue
- ✓ Embossing tool or bone folder
- ✓ Hole punch

one
Draw an 8cm (3¼in) square in the centre of the blue mottled card. Trace the template from page 115 and cut out. Draw a triangle on each side and cut out. Lay the template on the blue mottled card, mark the shape and cut out. Score across between the points of each V to make the square base. Punch a hole at the end of each point.

two
Sort out the white, pale blue and light turquoise flower sequins from the mixed pack. Stick flower sequins on the triangle points randomly, leaving the base clear. Stick a crystal bead over each flower sequin hole and some small sequins in between the flowers.

three
Thread a fine needle with some blue metallic thread. Pick up a bugle followed by a flower sequin. Repeat three more times and then pick up a seed bead. Missing out the seed bead, take the thread back up the flower sequins and bugles. Make a second string of beads. Tie the bead strands to one of the holes in the gift box so that the beads hang down like little tassels. Wrap the gift with tissue paper, place on the square base of the box and fold up the box points. Tie a loop of ribbon through the holes and into a bow, leaving long ends.

waxing lyrical

Make this sumptuous wrapping paper from waxed paper, sequins and beads for an extra special gift.

you will need...

✓ Translucent wax sandwich paper

✓ Silver star sequins

✓ Flat sequins 8mm (⁵⁄₁₆in) in blue and translucent

✓ Wide silver wire-edged ribbon to tie around the parcel

✓ Blue satin ribbon 30cm (12in) of 5mm (³⁄₁₆in) wide

✓ Selection of large silver beads

✓ Dressmaker's pins

one
Tear off two lengths of wax paper from the roll, large enough to wrap the parcel. Lay one piece on the ironing board, shiny side up and, if necessary, pin the corners to hold it flat.

two
Arrange star sequins all over the paper leaving gaps in between and then drop translucent and blue sequins randomly in between. Don't leave over-large gaps between sequins.

three
Carefully position the second piece of wax paper shiny side down, on top of the sequin-covered paper. Heat the iron to a medium heat and run the iron over the paper to melt the wax. You can keep ironing for a moment or two until the paper has a fairly even mottled appearance from the melted wax.

four
Leave the paper to cool and then use it to wrap the present. Think about how the parcel will be wrapped before beginning so you don't have to open out and refold the paper, as this will cause it to go cloudy along the folds.

five
Thread a selection of large beads on to the narrow ribbon and tie a knot at each end. Let half the beads drop down to each end. Tie the parcel with the wide silver ribbon, leaving the bow untied. Secure the narrow ribbon to where the ribbons cross so that the beads drop over the side. Tie the bow to finish.

try this
To make a matching gift tag, draw a star or other shape on wax paper, fill the area with sequins and lay another piece of wax paper on top. Iron the two layers with a medium heat. Sew around the design and then cut out and attach to a pretty tag.

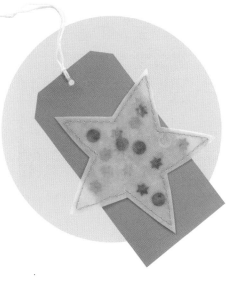

you will need...

✓ Wire 0.7mm (22 gauge) in peach, deep blue and turquoise

✓ Wire cutters and flat-nosed pliers

✓ Ice beads 8mm (⁵⁄₁₆in) and 10mm (³⁄₈in) in peach, dark blue and turquoise

✓ Sterling silver crimp-hook fastening

one To make the bracelet: Cut 1m (1yd) of peach wire and bend in half. Hold the bent end and twist until the wires are twisted for 10mm (³⁄₈in), leaving a loop at the end. Pick up a large peach ice bead on one wire.

quick & clever Enamelled wire is soft enough to be cut with a sturdy pair of craft or kitchen scissors – just cut as far away from the tips as possible for more leverage and to avoid damaging the blades.

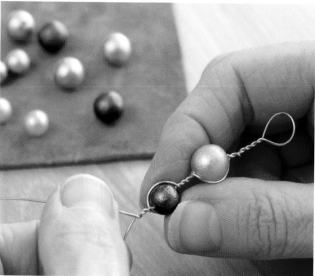

two Twist the wires together again for about 6mm (¼in) under the bead. Pick up a small deep blue bead on the shorter wire and twist again. Alternate colours of beads and sizes each time and keep adding the bead to the shorter wire (this changes each time). Continue adding beads with a section of twisted wire between until it is long enough to fit around your wrist.

three Working off the wire coil, wrap the end of a length of deep blue wire twice around the top of the bracelet. Bend the wire over the first bead at a different place than the peach wire and then wrap around the twisted wire section once. Continue down the bracelet in this way to the end and then wrap the wire around the bottom bead and cut off the excess.

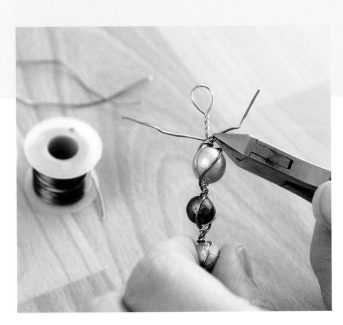

four Repeat this wrapping process with the turquoise wire so that the wires form a sort of cage over each bead. Once complete, trim both blue wires close to the twisted peach wire leaving at least 6mm (¼in) of twisted peach wire at each end.

five Finish the bracelet by trimming the peach wire so that it will fit into the sterling silver crimp fastening. The amount of wire to leave will depend on the particular fastening that you buy. You could twist a sample section of wire to test how much is required to fit inside the fastening so that it can be crimped securely before cutting the bracelet itself.

six To make the necklace: Cut about 2m (2¼yd) of wire and make the necklace in the same way as the bracelet. This style of necklace suits a slightly shorter length so that the wire moulds to the shape of your neck. Keep checking by trying the necklace on as you add beads until it is exactly the right length.

Craft wire is available in many colours, from rich burgundy and deep blue to funky lime and raspberry. Coloured enamelled wires come in a range of thicknesses, so you can create lots of different textures and effects. Bead shops usually stock a small range along with plain silver- and gold-plated wire but if you want something unusual refer to the suppliers on page 118.

superstar

Crimped wire is ideal for wrapping round cut shapes as the kinks help prevent the wire slipping. Some beads will simply hold in place because of the kinks in the wire – if not they can be secured by twisting the bead on the wire.

quick & clever If you can't find ready-made crimped wire you can feed wire through a paper-crimping tool to make your own.

you will need...

- ✓ Single-fold card 10 x 18cm (4 x 7in) in white creative hammer finish
- ✓ White glitter card
- ✓ Pink leather-effect paper
- ✓ Crimped silver-plated wire
- ✓ Small white flower beads, about ten
- ✓ Small white triangle beads, about ten
- ✓ Sheer crushed ribbon 25cm (10in) of 3.5cm (1½in) wide
- ✓ Double-sided tape and craft glue dots

one Trace the star template from page 113 and cut out a star in white glitter card. Cut a 50cm (20in) length of crimped wire and feed a triangle bead on one end. Wrap the end of the wire over the bead and above the bead to secure, then trim the tail.

two Pick up several flower and triangle beads alternately and twist to secure the first two along the length with a 1.5cm (⅝in) gap. Leave these beads as a tail and begin to wrap the wire around the star. Position and twist beads so that they are on the front of the star only. Wrap another two lengths of beaded wire around the star.

three Tear a 5cm (2in) wide band of pink leather-effect paper and cut to the length of the card. Wrap the ribbon over the paper and secure on the back of the paper and then stick the panel on the front of the card. Attach the star with craft glue dots or three-dimensional sticky fixers to add a little dimension.

cracking decoration

Make a set of opulent crackers to decorate the table for a dinner party or other special occasion. You can alter the colour of the foil, beads and wire to match your décor or choose colours to suit a particular occasion such as a wedding, christening or Christmas.

quick & clever Buy ready-made crackers and add the luxury touch with beaded wire and sheer organza ribbon.

you will need...

- ✓ A4 sheet of white mulberry paper
- ✓ A4 sheet of self-adhesive silver foil
- ✓ Cardboard tube 10cm (4in) long
- ✓ Silver-plated wire 0.5mm (25 gauge)
- ✓ Assortment of silver and silver-lined crystal beads
- ✓ Sheer burgundy ribbon 4cm (1½in) wide
- ✓ Double-sided tape

one Cut an 18 x 30cm (7 x 12in) piece of mulberry paper and lay on a flat surface. Cut two 6.5 x 18cm (2½ x 7in) pieces of self-adhesive silver foil and stick across each end.

two Cut a 10 x 18cm (4 x 7in) piece of silver foil and stick it centrally between the other two pieces. Lay the card tube on the reverse side on the central piece of foil, wrap around the tube and stick the foil with double-sided tape.

three Wrap a length of sheer burgundy ribbon around the cracker, fold in the raw edges and stick in place. Cut a 1.5m (1½yd) length of wire. Pick up a long bead and secure it about 15cm (6in) from the end by looping the wire back through the bead.

four Pick up a second smaller round or square bead and secure it about 2cm (¾in) away by twisting the bead on the wire to create a short stem. Add further pairs of beads with a 10–15cm (4–5in) gap between them. Make a second length of wire in the same way.

five Wrap one end of the beaded wire around the cracker to gather the mulberry paper. Wind the wire around the centre section of foil and then tie off the end by gathering the mulberry paper at the other side. Add the second length of beaded wire and finish the cracker by tying a ribbon bow at each end. Trim the ribbon ends attractively.

beads & ribbon

Using a few beads and sequins to embellish ribbons is one of the easiest ways to create an impression of lush beaded fabric.

ribbon patch cushion

Crazy patchwork is a traditional technique that has been updated here with ribbons and beads, all in scrumptious pinks. The easy-to-stitch patchwork is made up of squares and rectangles of fabric. Let the ribbons inspire the design – try adding beads along the picot edge of a ribbon or stitch beads in small areas such as flower centres or parts of a border pattern. You can buy ribbons individually but there are also packs available from craft shops in co-ordinated widths and colours. Finish the design with a few bead motifs, either ready-made or stitch your own. My cushion is approximately 30 x 40cm (12 x 16in).

right Select beads and fabric to match some pretty ribbons. You could also choose a colour theme for a special occasion, such as gold and ivory for a wedding ring pillow.

you will need...

- ✓ Sheets of plain paper for templates
- ✓ 0.5m (½yd) of 114cm (45in) wide fabric for main cushion front and back
- ✓ Small pieces of toning silk dupion and silk organza for the patchwork
- ✓ 1m (1yd) each of four differently coloured but co-ordinating ribbons

one Cut squares and rectangles of paper to lay out the patchwork, rearranging them until you are happy with the layout (see the small diagram below for my layout). Use these shapes as templates for cutting out the silk dupion and organza. Now iron the silk dupion and organza pieces on to fusible bonding web according to the manufacturer's instructions.

quick & clever When ironing on fusible bonding web use non-stick baking parchment to protect your iron, especially from organza.

two Cut a 32 x 42cm (12½ x 16½in) piece from the main fabric for the cushion front. Trim your silk dupion and organza patches if necessary, peel the backing paper off the bonding web and arrange the patches on the main cushion panel. Fuse the patches in place with a medium hot, dry iron.

three Arrange lengths of ribbon along the joins of the patchwork pieces and cut pieces to go across some of the patches. Once you are satisfied with the arrangement use narrow strips of fusible bonding web to attach the ribbon to the cushion front.

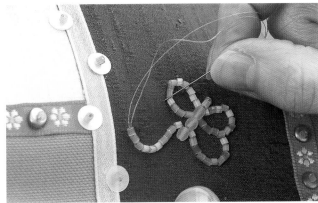

four Sew seed beads down each side of some of the strips of ribbon – this looks especially attractive if the ribbon has a picot edge. Use the pattern of other ribbons to guide where to attach other beads and sequins. Attach flat beads and sequins as follows: bring the thread up through the fabric, pick up a sequin and a seed bead, miss the seed bead and go back down though the sequin and the fabric.

five On one or two of the fabric patches embroider a small butterfly or other motif such as a flower. The butterfly shown here is created with three small oval beads for the body with seed beads forming the tail and antennae. Hex beads, which are rather like short bugles, are faceted to catch the light and make attractive wings. Couch the beads down every two or three beads to create the shape.

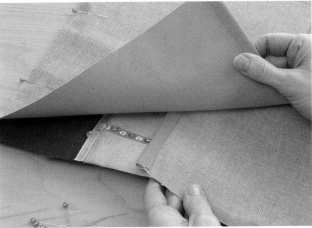

six To make the back of the cushion, cut two pieces of fabric 32 x 28cm (12½ x 11in). On one piece of fabric press under a 1cm (½in) turning on one long side and then fold over again to create a double hem. Repeat with the other piece of fabric and then machine stitch the hems.

seven With right sides together, pin one back piece along one edge of the main front panel. Pin the other back piece so that the hems overlap. Machine stitch around the outside edges of the cushion. Cut across the corners and turn through to the right side. Carefully press the cushion cover and insert a cushion pad to finish.

Ribbons are one of the easiest embellishments to buy and there is such a wide range of styles, materials and colours to choose from that you cannot fail to be inspired. Their gorgeous tactile quality contrasts so well with beads, which add texture and colour to any design. In order that the beads show up well keep any pattern on the ribbon fairly simple.

sheer and stunning

This pretty little gift bag made from an assortment of ribbons can be used for wedding favours or as a surprise gift for a special friend. Look for sheer ribbon with wire edges so it holds its shape and supports the bead embellishment.

you will need...

✓ Sheer wire-edge white ribbon 1m (1yd) of 6cm (2⅜in) wide

✓ White card 6cm (2⅜in) square

✓ Pale green satin ribbon 60cm (24in) of 3mm (⅛in) wide

✓ Dark green satin ribbon 30cm (12in) of 3mm (⅛in) wide

✓ Green wire 1m (1yd) of 0.5mm (25 gauge)

✓ Assortment of green beads and long bugles

one Cut the sheer ribbon into two equal lengths and lay them out so that they cross in the centre. Tuck the card between the layers and then sew around the edge to secure.

two Fold over a narrow turning then 6cm (2⅜in) at each end of the ribbon and sew running stitch along the edge of fold. Pull the stitches up to gather and sew the ends to secure. Tuck a small gift inside tissue paper and lay it in the centre. Lift up the sheer ribbons then tie the narrow satin ribbons around the neck.

three Take the green wire and pick up a bead. Wrap the wire around the bead and twist at the other end to secure. Add beads along the wire, twisting the wire to form a short stem and secure the bead. Wrap the wire loosely round the bag neck to finish.

polka placemat

A plain placemat for a table setting can be quickly transformed into something quite special with the addition of some pretty ribbon and a few well-placed beads. Choose ribbons that tone in with the colour of the mat and pick some pretty beads to match. Decorate a set of mats and matching coasters for a beautiful gift idea.

quick & clever If you are short of time just tie a bow of ribbon and attach to one corner of the placemat, sewing a few beads on it to embellish.

you will need...

✓ Green placemat 33 x 43cm (13 x 17in)

✓ Lime polka dot ribbon 40cm (16in) of 2.5cm (1in) wide

✓ Dark green ribbon 40cm (16in) x 2.5cm (1in) wide

✓ Assortment of green and white beads

✓ Sewing thread to match ribbons

✓ Dressmaker's pins

one Stitch the dark green ribbon down the left edge of the mat using small stitches and matching sewing thread. Lay the green polka dot ribbon on top and pin. Fold the end over to the reverse side at the top edge. Turn under the raw edges of both ribbons and sew neatly.

two Insert five pins along the length of the ribbons with 7cm (2¾in) gaps between. Gather the polka ribbon at each pin by oversewing with matching thread. Remove the pins.

quick & clever To achieve an instant party look for a festive table, use ribbon or trim in a fun, tactile texture, and sparkling beads in eye-catching finishes.

three Sew a selection of beads over the gathers to create pretty little clumps. Choose beads in a range of shapes and sizes to add interest – depending on the size you will need about seven at each gather.

four Fold the end of the ribbon over to the reverse side, turn under the raw edges and sew neatly to finish.

big beads

Big beads create instant impact – ideal for making chunky jewellery or adding eye-catching colour and texture quickly to a variety of designs.

turquoise tote

This stylish little bag is quick and easy to make and requires no special sewing skills because the seams are straight, with the shape created by a simple stitching technique. Add the beads of your choice to the specially designed wire handle or buy a ready-made beaded handle and attach it in the same way. Choose beads and fabric in your favourite colour but remember that the beads will show better against a plain fabric. PVC holds its shape well as it is fairly firm but if you choose a softer fabric, stiffen it by ironing fusible interfacing on the reverse side before sewing up. Insert a lining to finish the bag neatly. The bag shown is approximately 17 x 24cm (6¾ x 9½in) excluding handles.

right PVC fabric and plastic beads are fun for a young person, but you could use much more sophisticated beads and fabrics to create a more elegant design.

you will need...

✓ Turquoise PVC fabric 66 x 33cm
   (26 x 13in)

✓ Wire handles (see page 117)

✓ Chunky pony beads in gloss turquoise,
   frosted turquoise and frosted white

✓ Selection of interesting white and
   turquoise beads

✓ Silver-plated chain 76cm (30in)

quick & clever Attach chains of beads on a ready-made bag or hang them from your belt loops or favourite cardigan to make an attractive accessory.

one Cut two pieces of PVC fabric 33 x 31cm (13 x 12¼in). Lay them right sides together and machine stitch down the two shorter sides and along the bottom with 1.5cm (⅝in) seams. Open out the corners and position the side and bottom seams together. Pin through the seams without damaging the bag fabric. Measure in 7cm (2¾in) from the point and draw a perpendicular line across the corner. Machine stitch along this line and trim the seam to 6mm (¼in).

two Fold down the top edge by 1.5cm (⅝in) twice to form a double hem and hold it in place with paper clips. Pins and tacking (basting) are unsuitable for PVC fabric as the holes would look unsightly in the finished piece.

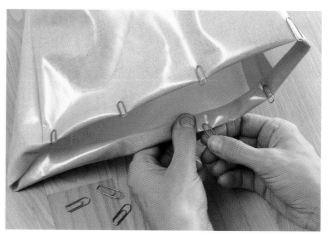

three Unscrew one end from the wire handles and feed on the pony beads. Alternate the colours and try to finish with the same colour at each end. You can slightly unscrew the first end so that you can squeeze on a last bead and then screw on the second end and tighten both securely.

quick & clever If you can't get the beads tightly packed on the wire handle add a thinner 'spacer' bead at each end.

✓ Small quantity of silver-plated wire 0.6mm (24 gauge)

✓ Silver-plated head pins

✓ Two lobster-claw clasps

✓ Three sets of jersey popper fasteners

✓ Round-nosed pliers, flat-nosed pliers and wire cutters

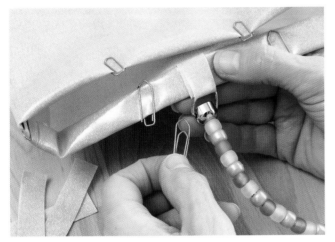

four Cut 8cm (3in) strips of PVC to fit through the handle loops. Position the first handle in the centre of one side. Fold the strips in half through the loops and then tuck the end under the hem so that the loop is at the top edge. Secure with a paper clip and secure the other end and the other handle in the same way.

quick & clever To help the bag hold its shape, cut stiff card to fit in the bag base, cover with PVC fabric and stick inside.

five Make a selection of bead charms to attach to a length of silver chain. Most beads can be attached using a head pin. Simply pick up one or more beads on the head pin and make a loop using round-nosed pliers. Trim off excess wire and straighten the loops with flat-nosed pliers. For other bead ideas see the instructions for the charm bracelet on page 60.

six Cut the chain to length so that the beads will hang inside the handle when it is down. Fit a lobster-claw clasp on each end and then attach the charms every three links or so along the length. Open the rings at the end of the head pin charms by pushing one end down.

seven Mark the position of the jersey poppers 2cm (¾in) either side of the side seams. Poppers have two separate parts that are secured using a special tool and a hammer. Fit a pair of poppers so the male and female side of the fastenings is on the outside, either side of the seam. Fit a second pair facing inwards in the middle of the handles, to close the bag.

Go into any bead shop and the first thing you notice is the wonderful array of beads laid out in trays ready for you to pick and choose. These beads are not necessarily particularly large but are definitely big enough to pick up individually. They are usually arranged by colour, which adds to the impact and makes selection a much easier process – although you may want to buy them all!

big and beautiful

Big beads are perfect for making a chunky-style necklace. To create an attractive, co-ordinated design choose an assortment of beads in a simple colourway but select mixed sizes, shapes and textures to add interest. Thread the beads on monofilament or fine waxed cotton and attach the best quality fastening to make a really stunning necklace.

quick & clever Choose a chunky necklace fastening, rather than something delicate, to balance the size of the beads.

you will need...

✓ Assortment of large beads, about 40cm (16in) total length
✓ Monofilament
✓ Toggle necklace fastening

quick & clever A bead length of 40cm (16in) makes a good short necklace – for a longer necklace simply add more beads.

one Tie a 60cm (24in) length of monofilament on to one part of the necklace fastening by wrapping the end around several times and tying off with several double half hitch knots (see the diagram below).

two Thread a long narrow bead on to the filament and tuck the tail through the bead and trim the end. If you have no narrow beads use 5–6 seed beads at each end instead, so that the fastening can be undone. Pick up a selection of beads until the necklace is the length required.

three Make sure the last bead is quite narrow and then tie on the other part of the necklace, fastening as before. Thread the tail back through one or two beads and snip off the end.

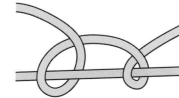

double half-hitch knot

summery sandals

That basic of the summer wardrobe, a pair of flip-flops, can be made into something quite special with the addition of a quick bead embellishment. Choose some pretty, big beads in a matching colour to make a quick star shape.

quick & clever For a temporary beady look stick the bead embellishments in place with a few large craft glue dots.

you will need...

- ✓ Pair of sandals or flip-flops
- ✓ Pink wire 0.7mm (22 gauge)
- ✓ Twenty-four pony beads 3mm (⅛in)
- ✓ Assortment of big beads in pinks and red
- ✓ Round-nosed pliers and wire cutters
- ✓ Epoxy resin glue

one Cut a length of pink wire and wrap the end around some round-nosed pliers (or a fine knitting needle) to make a short spring. Trim off the tail end.

two Pick up a pony bead and then 5 or 6 beads larger beads in a range of shapes and sizes. Pick up another pony bead and wrap the wire around the pliers again to make a short spring at the other end. Make another two beaded wires in the same way.

three Lay the beaded wires so they overlap in the middle of the beads. Wrap a second length of wire around where they cross to secure, leaving two long ends. Pick up 2 or 3 larger beads on each end and then a pony bead and secure with a spring as before. Trim off the tail of the wire. Wrap another piece of wire around the middle and add fewer beads to create the 'centre' of the flower.

four Make a second bead embellishment for the other sandal. Attach the beads to the strap using a strong adhesive such as epoxy resin.

beads & metal foil

Metal foil can be cut with scissors, embossed and shaped to make a wide range of motifs and backgrounds for beads and sequins.

jester candleholder

The simple design of this candleholder can easily be adapted for a range of candle sizes. The outer layer of foil is medium weight so it holds its shape and supports the lighter weight coloured foil inside. The holder has also been designed so that the candle can be lifted out when it has burnt down too far and replaced with a new candle. You could create little beaded motifs on the foil or go for the simple band of beads shown here. To make sure the beads stay securely stuck to the foil use hi-tack tape, sold in a range of different widths especially for this purpose.

right The snowflake pattern on the metal foil makes this candle ideal on a winter table setting but you could draw hearts on red foil instead for a romantic dinner for two.

you will need...

✓ Medium-weight aluminium foil
✓ Lightweight blue foil
✓ Wooden embossing tool

✓ Mixed seed beads in blue and turquoise
✓ Medium silver accent beads
✓ Ten teardrop beads
✓ Hi-tack tape 1.25cm (½in) wide
✓ Candle 8cm (3in) diameter approx

quick & clever The candle-holder can be stored from one year to the next if you uncurl the metal foil so that it is flat against the candle and then wrap the whole item in tissue paper.

one Cut a 10cm (4in) wide strip of paper to fit around your candle. Fold the paper into five equal sections and mark the centre point of each section at one side. Draw triangles and cut out. (You can use the template provided on page 115 if your candle is 8cm (3in) diameter.)

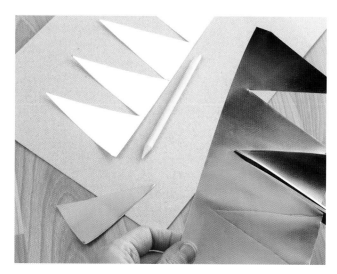

two Position the paper template 1.25cm (½in) from the edge of the aluminium foil and draw around the points with a fine embossing tool (or use an old ball-point pen that's run out of ink). Cut out, including the tab on the bottom edge at one end (shown in the next picture).

three Stick hi-tack tape along the bottom edge of the foil panel, leaving the tab clear. Remove the backing tape. Pour the mixed seed beads into a shallow tray. Hold the panel in the tin and then shake the beads over the tape until as many as possible have stuck. Change the beads for silver accent beads and repeat the process to fill in the gaps between the seed beads. Shake off any loose beads.

✓ Silver-plated wire

✓ Round-nosed pliers and wire cutters

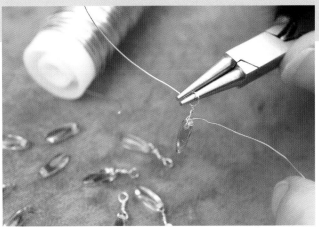

four Lay the foil panel on a piece of soft card or foam sheet. Using a wooden embossing tool, draw freehand motifs such as snowflakes, swirls or little hearts over each triangle from the beaded side. To draw snowflakes, draw a simple six-point star and then a V shape on each arm.

quick & clever Rub the embossing tool into the candle base before drawing on the foil and it will glide over the surface more easily.

five To make the teardrop charms, feed a length of fine silver wire through the hole in a teardrop bead. Twist the ends of the wire together for 6mm (¼in) and then make a ring on one of the 'tails' of wire close to the twist. Wind the wire tail back down around the twist and trim the ends. Make ten charms in total.

six Cut a foil panel in blue foil in the same way as before, remembering the tab at one end. Wrap the foil panel around the candle and stick the tab on the outside. Use a few small pieces of double-sided tape to secure the aluminium foil on top and stick the tab on the inside this time.

seven Shape the foil triangles by curving gently over your fingers. Attach a teardrop charm on the end of each triangle. To do this, simply fold the point underneath and hook the ring on the teardrop charm over.

Metal foil is available in a range of thicknesses but for the projects in this book I have avoided very heavy sheets as these need a different marking technique that requires a punch tool and hammer. Medium-weight foil is generally only available in aluminium, pewter, bronze, copper and gold whereas lightweight foils are also sold in a range of bright colours. Stick beads on to the foil using multi-surface paints, strong glue that dries clear or hi-tack tape.

shiny stocking

A simple foil bookplate decorated with pretty beads and sequins turns a simple suede notebook into something quite special. Use this Christmas design to keep a record of addresses for cards and presents, or try creating your own design for an address book, wedding album or guest list.

quick & clever Use multi-surface paints, which come in handy bottles with a fine nozzle, for sticking the beads – it's more secure than glue.

you will need...

- ✓ Deep red suede notebook 15 x 21.5cm (6 x 8½in)
- ✓ Lightweight aqua and aluminium (silver) foil
- ✓ Seed beads in aqua, deep pink and deep turquoise
- ✓ Star sequins in aqua, deep pink and deep turquoise
- ✓ Foam sheet
- ✓ Wooden embossing tool
- ✓ Aqua pearl multi-surface paint
- ✓ Double-sided tape
- ✓ Craft glue dots

one Trace the stocking template from page 113 and cut out. Lay the aqua foil on a sheet of foam or folded newspaper and draw around the template using a wooden embossing tool. Lift off the template, draw zigzag patterns on the top part of the stocking and carefully cut out the stocking shape.

two Cut a 9 x 12cm (3½ x 4¾in) panel from aqua foil and a 7 x 10cm (2¾ x 4in) panel from aluminium foil. Draw simple star patterns on the aluminium foil and mark dots in between. Using double-sided tape, stick the stocking to the aluminium panel and then stick the whole panel on to the aqua panel.

three Using multi-surface paint, stick aqua seed beads on the dots on the aluminium panel and star sequins on the corners of the aqua panel. With the embossing tool, mark straight lines around the aqua border then stick the main panel to the notebook. Cut or punch large stars from aluminium foil and stick around the panel using craft glue dots. Decorate the stocking with star sequins and seed beads to finish.

swinging 60s

Templates are an ideal way to create shapes from foil. You can buy plastic templates in lots of different themes or draw your own. This girly theme is a super way to send special wishes to friend or for an invite to a summer soirée or cocktail party.

you will need...

✓ A4 sheet of red card

✓ Pink circle vellum

✓ Lightweight foil in red and aqua

✓ Wooden embossing tool

✓ Red seed beads

✓ Multi-surface paint in pink crystal

✓ Vellum adhesive

✓ Heart punch

✓ Double-sided tape

one Cut a 20 x 15cm (8 x 6in) piece of red card, score down the centre and fold in half to make a 10 x 15cm (4 x 6in) single-fold card. Cut a 10 x 15cm (4 x 6in) piece of pink circle vellum. Apply vellum adhesive to the front of the card and then stick the vellum panel on to it.

two Trace the dress template from page 114 and cut out. Lay the aqua foil on a foam sheet and draw around the template with a wooden embossing tool. Lift off the paper template and draw in the decoration on the dress, including the indentations for the seed beads.

three Cut out the dress and stick on the front of the card using double-sided tape. Draw a thin line of multi-surface paint along the neckline and dress border. Drop red seed beads into the paint to create a solid line. Stick red seed beads in the dents on the dress.

four Punch nine or ten hearts from the red side of the foil and another five from the silver side of the foil (the foil domes slightly depending on how it is fitted into the punch). Use multi-surface paint to stick these hearts around the dress to finish.

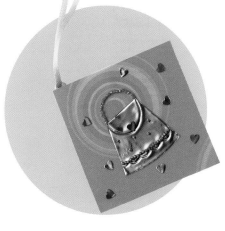

trythis
If you are short of time just make this little handbag as a mini card or pretty tag to attach to a gift. Cut red card 7.5 x 15cm (3 x 6in). Score and fold down the centre. Stick a piece of circle vellum on the front using vellum adhesive. Trace the template from page 114 and use to make a handbag. Stick the foil bag on the card and decorate with red seed beads. Draw a handle shape with multi-surface paint and fill in with red seed beads. Decorate the card front with red and silver foil hearts. Punch a hole on the inside and thread through a length of ribbon.

templates

All templates are shown actual size, ready to trace.

Fab flowers album (page 40)

Purple passion (page 56)

Superstar (page 92)

Shooting star (page 57)

Shiny stocking (page 110)

Fun felt box (page 45)

Heart's desire (page 81)

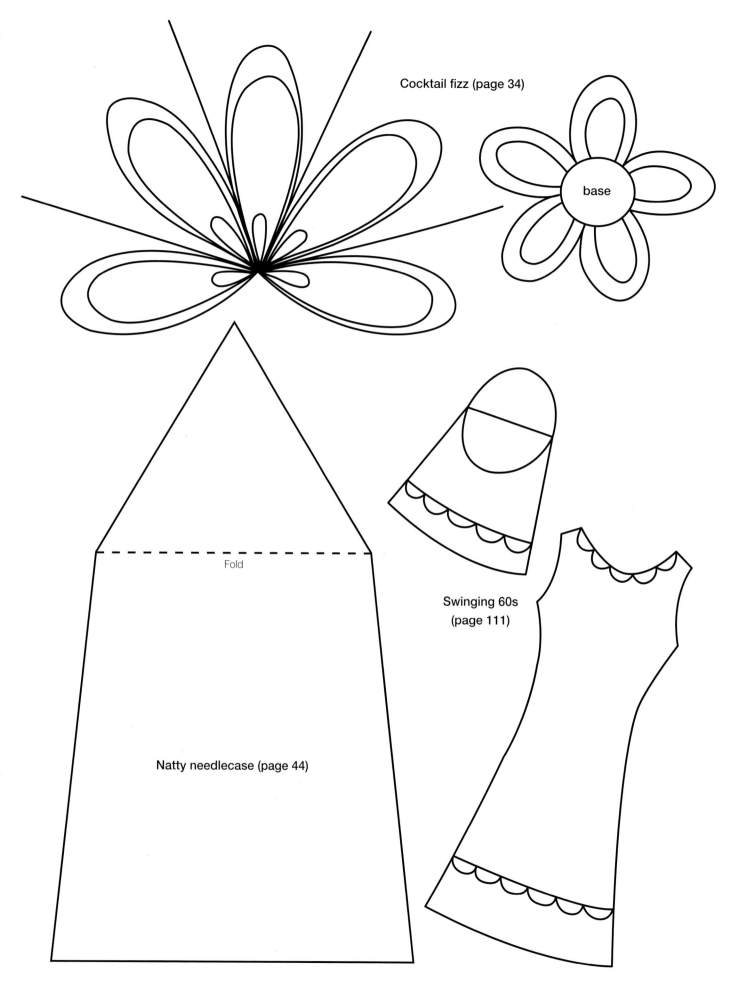

Cocktail fizz (page 34)

base

Fold

Swinging 60s
(page 111)

Natty needlecase (page 44)

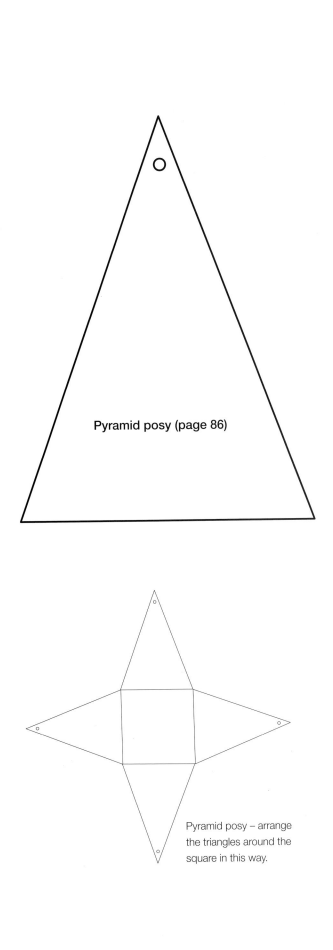

Pyramid posy (page 86)

Pyramid posy – arrange
the triangles around the
square in this way.

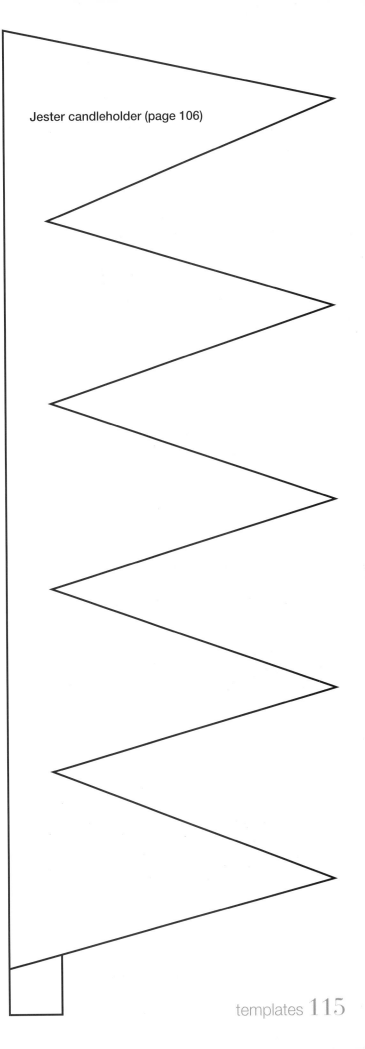

Jester candleholder (page 106)

project product details

This list contains details of the various materials and products used in the projects (available at the date of publication) – see Suppliers on page 118 for contact details.

Beaded fruit (page 18)
Pear shapes – from your local florist
Pearls on strings – Creative Beadcraft
Hi-tack tape – Knorr Prandell

Round 'n' round (page 20)
Bead strings – The Viking Loom
Hi-tack sheet – Knorr Prandell

Scatter cushion (page 24)
Bead fringing – John Lewis

Sweet heart (page 26)
Bead fringing – John Lewis
Silk and netting – John Lewis
Heart buttons – Crafts U Love

Sheer 'n' swinging (page 27)
Bead fringing – John Lewis
Silk and organza – James Hare Silks

Dolly bag (page 30)
Silk dupion – James Hare Silks
Sequin trimming – Hobbycraft

Funky frame (page 32)
Bead trim – V V Rouleaux
Silk – John Lewis

Shades of apricot (page 33)
Bead trim – V V Rouleaux
Sinamay – John Lewis

Cocktail fizz (page 36)
Multi-surface paints (Pebéo touch) – Hobbycraft

Sparkly bauble (page 38)
Multi-surface paint (Pebéo touch) – Hobbycraft
Beads and sequins (Gütermann) – Hobbycraft

Dotty greetings (page 39)
Backing paper (Sophie collection)
  – Cotswold Keepsakes
Beads and sequins (Gütermann) – Hobbycraft

Fab flowers album (page 42)
Bead selection – The Viking Loom
Bone beads – The Spellbound Bead Company
Ribbon (Making Memories) – Memory Keepsakes

Natty needlecase (page 44)
Star sequins (Gütermann) – Hobbycraft
Blue wax cotton thread – Creative Beadcraft

Fun felt box (page 45)
Bugles and seed beads (Gütermann) – The Bead Shop
Square beads – The Bead Shop

Plaited necklace (page 48)
Seven-strand tigertail – The Spellbound Bead Company
Jewellery findings – The London Bead Company
Bead selection – Hobbycraft
Wire mesh and organza ribbons – Ribbon Designs

Thanks for the memory (page 50)
Bracelet memory wire – The Spellbound Bead Company
Bead selection – The Spellbound Bead Company
Memory wire ball ends – Constellation Beads

Turquoise and lime duo (page 51)
Seven-strand tigertail, beads and jewellery findings
  – The Spellbound Bead Company

Polka dot box (page 54)
Fimo polymer clay – Hobbycraft
Seed beads – Hobbycraft

Purple passion (page 56)
Fimo polymer clay – Hobbycraft
Seed beads – Hobbycraft
Ceramic washer beads – Creative Beadcraft

Shooting star (page 57)
Fimo polymer clay – Hobbycraft
Beads and key ring fitment – Hobbycraft
Tigertail – The Spellbound Bead Company

Charm bracelet (page 60)
Silver-plated chain bracelet – Claire's Accessories
Beads and findings – The Spellbound Bead Company
Long crystal bugles – Creative Beadcraft

Kilt pin (page 62)
Kilt pin – Tout à Loisirs
Bead selection – Tout à Loisirs
Jump rings and wire – Hobbycraft

Luscious links (page 63)
Bead selection – The Viking Loom
Wire and jewellery findings – Hobbycraft

Sequin flower bag (page 66)
Silk dupion – James Hare silks
Sequin flower motifs – Coats Crafts

suppliers

UK AND EUROPE

Claire's Accessories
Throughout Europe and USA, for nearest store:
email: customerservice@claires.com
www.claires.co.uk
(For charm bracelet and bead accessories)

Coats Crafts UK
PO Box 22, Lingfield Point, Darlington,
Co. Durham DL1 12YQ
tel: 01325 394237
email: consumer.ccuk@coats.com
www.coatscrafts.com
(For metallic threads and stranded cotton)

Constellation Beads
PO Box 88, Richmond, North Yorkshire DL10 4FT
tel: 01748 826552
email: info@constellationbeads.co.uk
www.constellationbeads.co.uk
(For beads and beading supplies)

Cotswold Keepsakes
The Parlour Workshop, Osney Hill Farm, North Leigh,
Witney, Oxfordshire OX29 6PJ
tel: 01993 700246
email: mail@cotswoldkeepsakes.co.uk
www.cotswoldkeepsakes.co.uk
(For cardmaking supplies)

Craft Creations
Ingersoll House, Delamare Road, Cheshunt,
Hertfordshire EN8 9HD
tel: 01992 781900
email: enquiries@craftcreations.com
www.craftcreations.com
(For card blanks, cardstock, double-sided tape)

Crafts U Love
Three Pines, 170 Balcombe Road, Horley,
Surrey RH6 9ER
tel: 01293 776465
email: enquiries@craftsulove.co.uk
www.craftsulove.co.uk
(For buttons and cardmaking supplies)

Crafty Ribbons
3 Beechwood, Clump Farm, Tin Pot Lane,
Blandford, Dorset DT11 7TD
tel: 01258 455889
email: info@craftyribbons.com
www.craftyribbons.com
(For mixed packs of ribbons)

Cranberry Cards
16 Dyffryn Business Park, Ystrad Mynach,
Hengoed, Wales CF82 7RJ
tel: 01443 819319
www.cranberrycards.co.uk
*(For cardmaking supplies, including
nine-circles aperture card)*

Creative Beadcraft
20 Beak Street, London W1R 3HA
tel: 0207 6299964
Mail order tel: 01494 778818
email: beads@creativebeadcraft.co.uk
www.creativebeadcraft.co.uk
(For beads and beading supplies)

Hobbycraft Superstores (stores throughout UK)
Help Desk, The Peel Centre, St Ann Way, Gloucester,
Gloucestershire GL1 5SF
For nearest store tel: 0800 027 2387
Mail order tel: 01202 596100
www.hobbycraft.co.uk
(For a huge range of craft supplies)

John Lewis (stores throughout UK)
tel: 08456 049 049
www.johnlewis.com
(For fabric, bead trimmings, beads, haberdashery)

James Hare Silks
PO Box 72, Monarch House, Queen Street,
Leeds LS1 1LX
tel: 0113 243 1204
www.jamesharesilks.co.uk
(For silk dupion and organza)

Josy Rose
PO Box 44204, London E3 3XB
tel: 0845 450 1212
email: info@josyrose.com
www.josyrose.com
(For bead trims)

Kleins
5 Noel Street, London W1F 8GD
tel: 0207 437 6162
email: mail@kleins.co.uk
www.kleins.co.uk
(For beads and bag handles)

Knorr Prandell and Gütermann
Perivale-Gütermann Ltd, Bullsbrook Road,
Middlesex UB4 OJR
tel: 0208 8589 1624
(For beads, hi-tack tape and accent beads)

LJ Gibbs and Partners
Bluebell Farm, Hewitts Road, Orpington,
Kent BR6 7QR
tel: 01959 533663
email: info@ljgibbsandpartners.com
www.ljgibbsandpartners.com
(For wire and handmade paper)

Memory Keepsakes
Shakeford Mill, Hinstock, Market Drayton,
Shropshire TF9 2SP
tel: 01630 638342
email: sales@memorykeepsakes.co.uk
www.memorykeepsakes.co.uk
(For cardmaking supplies)

Paper Cellar
Parkville House, Red Lion Parade, Pinner,
Middlesex HA5 3RR
tel: 08718713711
email: contact@papercellar.com
www.papercellar.com
(For paper and cardmaking supplies)

Ribbon Designs
PO Box 382, Edgware, Middlesex HA8 7XQ
tel: 0208 958 4966
email: info@silkribbon.co.uk
(For wire mesh and organza ribbon)

Shawes Arts & Craft Centre
68–70 Mansfield Road, Nottingham NG1 3GY
tel: 0115 941 8646
Or call Royal Sovereign for nearest stockist
tel: 0208 888 6888
(For art emboss foil)

The Bead Shop
104–106 Upper Parliament Street,
Nottingham NG1 6LF
tel: 0115 9588899
email: info@mailorder-beads.co.uk
www.mailorder-beads.co.uk
(For beads and findings)

The London Bead Company
339 Kentish Town Road, London NW5 2TJ
tel: 0870 203 2323
email: londonbead@dial.pipex.com
www.londonbeadco.co.uk
(For beads and findings)

The Spellbound Bead Company
45 Tamworth Street, Lichfield
Staffordshire WS13 6JW
tel: 01543 417650
www.spellboundbead.co.uk
(For beads and findings)

The Viking Loom
22 High Petergate, York YO1 7EH
tel: 01904 765599
email: vikingloom@vikingloom.co.uk
www.vikingloom.co.uk
(For bead strings and bead mixes)

Tout à Loisirs
50 Rue des Archives, Paris 75004
tel: 01 48 87 08 87
www.toutaloisirs.fr
(For kilt pins and beads)

V V Rouleaux
54 Sloane Square, London SW1W 8AX
tel: 0207730 3125
email: general@vvrouleaux.com
www.vvrouleaux.com
(For ribbons and bead trims)

USA

Beadbox
1290 N. Scottdale Road, Tempe, AZ 85821-1703
tel: 480 967-4080
www.beadbox.com
(For beads and findings)

Joann
2361 Rosecrans Ave, Suite 360, El Segundo, CA 90245
tel: 1-800-525-4951
www.joann.com
(For beads, bag handles and general craft supplies)

M & J Trimmings
1008 Sixth Avenue, New York, NY 10018
tel: 212 204 9595
www.mjtrim.com
(For beads, buttons, ribbons and trimmings)

acknowledgments

Many thanks to the following companies for so generously supplying materials for the book: Coats Crafts, Cotswold Keepsakes, Craft Creations, Crafts U Love, Crafty Ribbons, Josy Rose, Knorr Prandell, LJ Gibbs and Partners, Memory Keepsakes, Perivale-Gütermann, Ribbon Designs and Woodware.

Thanks to the editorial team, especially Cheryl who has given tremendous support and to Jennifer for her great organization. Special thanks to Lin for her usual professional work in editing the text. Thanks to Ginette for the super photography and to art editor Prudence, who has designed such a lovely book and to Ali Sharland who allowed us to take over her home near Stroud for a couple of days for photography. Finally, thanks to Louise Smythson who worked with me and assisted on several of the projects.

about the author

Dorothy Wood is a talented and prolific craft maker and author. Since completing a course in Advanced Embroidery and Textiles at Goldsmith's College, London, she has written over 20 craft books, and contributed to many others, on all kinds of subjects. This is Dorothy's fifth book published by David & Charles, her first being the best-selling *Simple Glass Beading*, plus *Simply Sensational Beading* and *Beautiful Beaded Bags*. She also contributes to several well-known craft magazines, including *Crafts Beautiful*, *Quick and Crafty* and *Cardmaking & Papercrafts*. Dorothy lives in the small village of Osgathorpe, Leicestershire, UK.

index

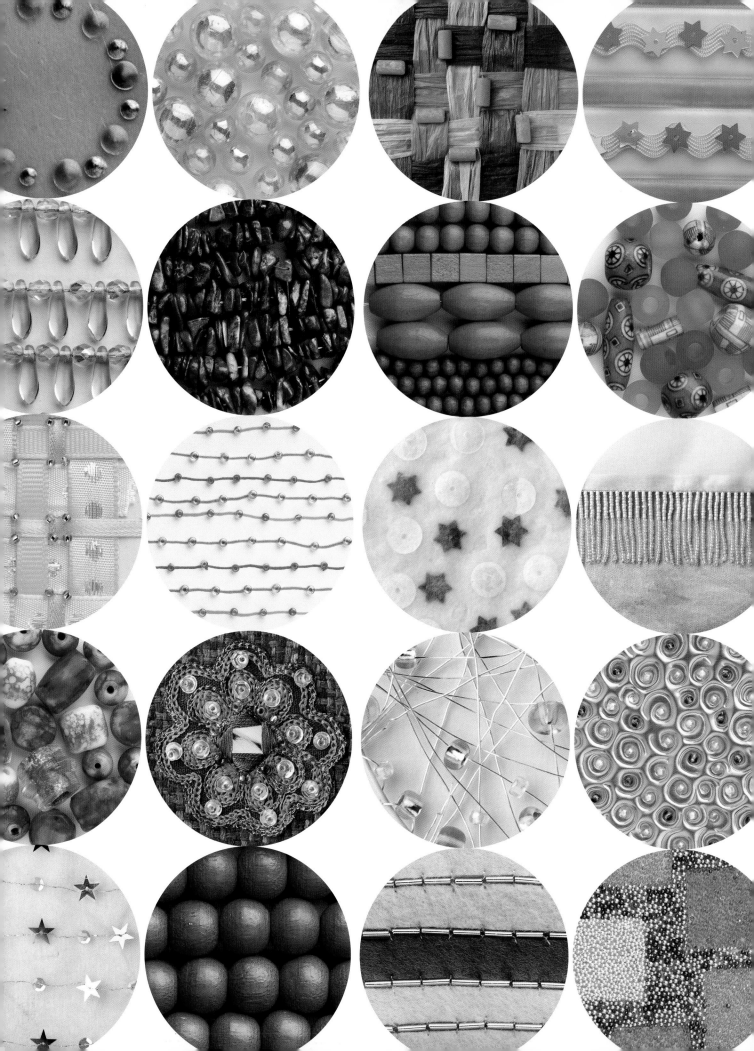

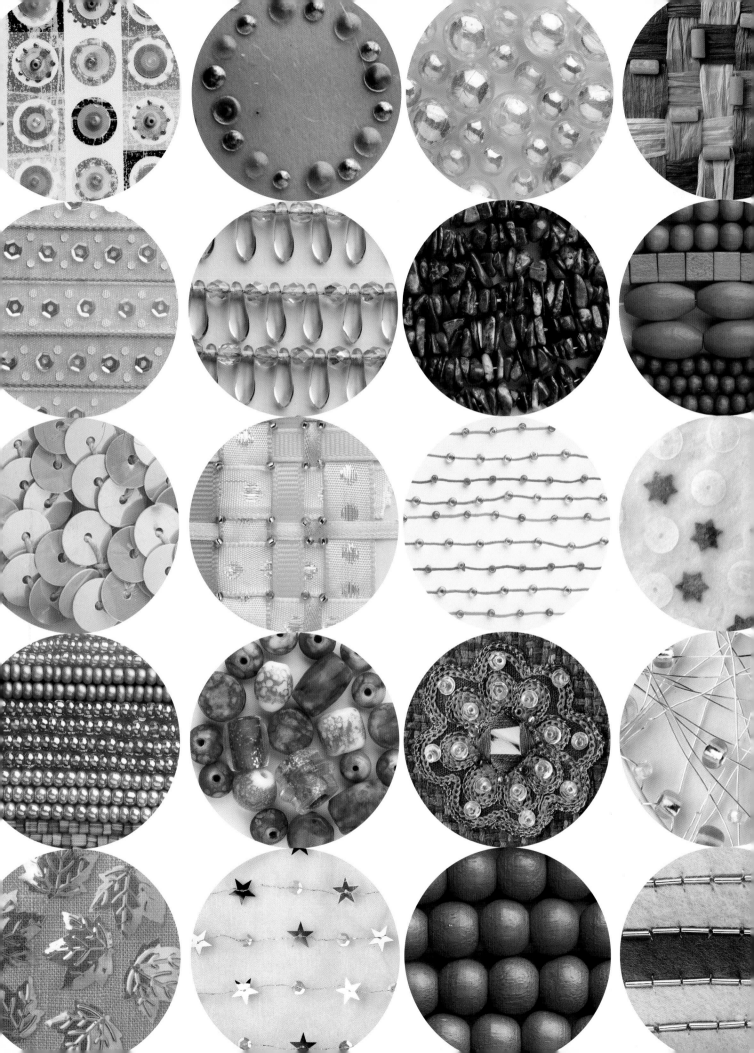